HERE'S WHAT I THINK

HERE'S WHAT I THINK

GWEN C. SCHALL

PALMETTO
PUBLISHING
Charleston, SC
www.PalmettoPublishing.com

Copyright © 2024 by Gwen C. Schall

All rights reserved
No portion of this book may be reproduced, stored in a retrieval system, or transmitted in any form by any means–electronic, mechanical, photocopy, recording, or other–except for brief quotations in printed reviews, without prior permission of the author.

Paperback ISBN: 979-8-8229-3720-8

Dedication

I dedicate this memoir to my husband, Perry, who has always supported me through some of my toughest times and has shown me what it means to love; to my children, Leslie and Elliot who continuously amaze me with all their accomplishments and shower me with unconditional love; and my brothers, Steven and Rick, whose lives have helped shape who I am.

TABLE OF CONTENTS

Preface 1
1. The Demise of Etty G 3
2. Meeting Jesus in Heaven 25
3. Mastectomy 33
4. Where Is Home 41
5. The Worst Pain 53
6. A Conflicted Soul 57
7. The Art of Teaching 67
8. Family 77

PREFACE

This memoir was written to give my readers an idea of my early life growing up in New York and how I evolved into adulthood. It includes sad, challenging, and happy times. Life is truly a journey, and it's worth looking back to ensure a brighter future.

Writing this memoir gave me a chance to look back at some of the events that have had an impact on me. I am sharing these experiences and thoughts with you so you can take a look at what I think. I need to express my views and what I have come away with in shaping my own life.

I was inspired to write my memoir after reading my good friend Sandra Rosenbloom's memoir. During the summer of 2022, I took an online course on how to write a memoir. It helped me get started, and from there I was able to develop my own style of how I wanted to express some of the important events in my life.

I dedicate this memoir to my husband Perry and my children, Leslie and Elliot. With their love and support, I am able to face many of life's challeges. I am grateful to my two brothers, Steven and Rick, for helping me get my facts accurate and for being a big part of my life.

THE DEMISE OF ETTY G

▷ ○ ☐ △ ▷

Who is Etty G? She is Elaine Green, Yiddish name Ethyl. She was born in Brooklyn, New York, in 1931 and grew up in Brighton Beach. She was the queen of the Coney Island handball courts and a graduate of Lincoln High School.

Her parents, Anna and Julius, were Russian immigrants who arrived in the U.S. through Ellis Island to escape the pogroms and the Russian Revolution between 1917 and 1923. They settled into life on the Lower East Side of Manhattan and later moved to Oceanside on Long Island. They eventually found themselves in Brooklyn, where Julius got a job delivering baked goods. He worked the night shift, from about 10:00 p.m. to about 7:00 a.m. This meant he would sleep most of the day. Anna, who was fluent in Hebrew and Yiddish, taught at a small Yeshiva down the street from where they were living.

On January 21, 1925, they had a son, Charlie. He was born on the kitchen table and weighed over nine pounds. Anna had a terrible delivery, claiming it tore her up. She vowed never to have any more children. As it turned out, Julius and Anna ended up taking in Anna's sister Charlotte's son, Carl, when Charlotte died unexpectedly from an ectopic pregnancy. Carl's father was on the road a lot and could not care for his young son.

So Anna and Julius raised him as their own child. But Julius wanted more children and threatened to divorce Anna if she didn't.

So reluctantly, Anna gave birth to Elaine seven years later, on July 14th, 1931. Julius adored his daughter. She was his companion to the Brooklyn Dodgers games, Saturday morning synagogue services, and Sunday walks for bagels and knishes.

Then, at around eight years old, Elaine developed nephritis and was bedridden for almost a year. This caused her to lose a whole year in school. After recovering, she needed to be held back. As disappointed as she was, she found friends who would end up being her friends for life. Later, while in high school, these same friends formed a group and called themselves "The Amigos."

Elaine Green was my mother. She claimed living by the ocean was the best part of growing up in Brighton Beach. Elaine and her friends spent much of their free time walking on the boardwalk. On weekends during the hot summer months, they would throw down their blankets and lay on the beach in their fashionable one-piece swim suites.

After graduating from high school in 1950, she registered for classes at Brooklyn College and took a part-time secretarial job. Then sometime that year, she and the Amigos were walking on the boardwalk. Lo and behold, they came upon a group of sailors. One in particular flirted with her, and she was so taken by him that she gave him her phone number.

They dated for a short time. She wanted to marry him and ended up dropping out of college. On June 23rd, 1951, Elaine Green married Murray Antonoff.

They first rented an apartment across from Ebbets Field, home of the Dodgers, in Brooklyn. Murray worked with his parents in their upholstery shop. Elaine became a homemaker. The apartment was small, and when Elaine became pregnant in the fall of 1952, they moved to a home in Bergen Beach. I was born the following June 1953. Two years later, my brother Steven was born. Then, in 1956, she found herself pregnant again, and in May 1957, Rick was brought into the world. Elaine enjoyed raising her three young children. Her parents would often come by to help her out.

Murray, in the meantime, was feeling the urge to expand his parents' business and started selling dinette sets. He moved the family to Far Rockaway, Queens, in 1958. He purchased a two-family home on Camp Road. Being a savvy businessman, he figured that renting the upstairs would help him offset his monthly mortgage payments. His parents were still involved in the business, and as it was expanding, he moved it into a larger space. He began bringing in wrought iron furniture, which was very much in demand. When the children were all in school, Elaine was asked to come into the store and help with the bookkeeping. It was a tough time for her. Murray's parents, Sam and Nora, were always looking over her shoulders and would make condescending remarks. They appeared suspicious of her and made her life difficult. She would often complain to me about how horribly they treated her. She just couldn't understand why they would be like this when her parents were always loving toward Murray. It was about this time that Elaine developed psoriasis on both elbows.

The public school system in our area was going on split session, which meant younger students were to attend school from 7:30 a.m. and leave at 12:30 p.m. The older students were to come to classes at 1:00 p.m. and get dismissed at 4:00 p.m. To make it easier for Elaine to work, our parents enrolled us in a Jewish day school that started at 8:00 a.m. and ended at 4:00 p.m. She was not happy, and neither were we. We tried to make it work. But Murray realized he needed to get away from his parents. Finally, he found two men who would be interested in starting a new furniture store, primarily selling wrought iron dinette sets. After cutting ties with his parents, money was tight as these three men were in the early stages of creating what would later become Antarenni. My mother had to help out financially, so she took a job at an orthodox day camp in Far Rockaway called Camp Holiday. She drove the van that picked up all the campers and then would work in the kitchen, preparing lunch for all the campers. Luckily, growing up with a somewhat orthodox father, she knew all the laws of Kashrut. The perk of getting the job was that all three of us children could attend for free.

Then, in 1964, our family once again moved. This time we moved out to Cedarhurst on Long Island. It was a small town, but it was part of a group of towns known as the Five Towns. It was a pretty affluent area. I remembered that before moving there, my parents looked at homes in Oceanside and Great Neck. My father was finally making a nice income, and my mother wanted to live in the suburbs. When I look back at this now, I feel she wanted to flaunt her rise in wealth, and that gave her ego a boost.

Elaine no longer had to work. She was a stay-at-home mom, which was exactly what she wanted to be. Our home was a modest split level, and all the neighbors knew each other. My parents often went out with the other couples in the neighborhood.

Although my father was far from being a religious man, my mother had us join the Sephardic Temple that was three blocks up the road from where we lived. Both my brothers had their bar mitzvahs there. I liked going just to check out the social scene, including checking out the cute guys. Unfortunately, girls and boys sat separately, so I don't think any boys there noticed me. Even though my mother was not considered orthodox, she was pretty observant. She'd pack away all the bread products during Passover and never let us attend school on Rosh

Hashanah or Yom Kippur. On Friday nights we always went to Brooklyn to have a Friday night meal with her parents. Her father ended up having prostate cancer that metastasized into his colon. He had to have a colostomy and needed to wear a colostomy bag. He was bedridden for several months. Julius passed away when he was sixty-five.

With the business growing, my father, who was in charge of sales, would often have to travel and spend several evenings away from home. Anna would come and stay with us. She kept her apartment in Brighton Beach, the same one my mother grew up in. Anna loved going across the street to the baths and playing canasta with her friends. She passed away at the age of seventy-four while I was in college. Interestingly, my mother always blamed Carl for Anna's death. He was scheduled to pick up my grandmother to take her to his home for the weekend. When he showed up to get her, she didn't answer the door, so he thought she had gone across the street to the baths and had forgotten he was coming for her, and he left. She was later found dead on her bed. She had apparently suffered a heart attack. My mother stopped talking to Carl after that.

A funny thing about my father was how he loved to work with his hands. He started driving Cadillacs, and on weekends he would be found in the garage working on his car or my mother's. This was a big thing. My family was able to afford two cars. Elaine's first car was a Rambler. I vaguely remember my father having to teach her how to drive. After a few years, she wanted a convertible, so my father got her a Falcon convertible. She loved that car. When either car had a problem, it never went into a shop for repairs; Murray knew how to fix it.

Another huge passion my father had was his love for dogs. My mother grew to love them too. As long as I can remember, we always had a dog in the house. The two she was most fond of were the boxer, Corky, who had eight puppies, and the Airedale, Curly. We always had female dogs because my parents felt they would be better with children. I think the dogs were my mother's companions while she was home alone. It gave her purpose as we three kids got older and more independent, doing our own things.

There were good family times, like when we made car trips down to Florida or spent time at a bungalow colony in the Catskills. I remember the vacation we took to Lake Hopatcong in New Jersey and the long road trip up to Montreal to see the World's Fair, known as Expo 67.

Then, around 1968, something drastic started to happen in my family. My parents came back from a trip to Acapulco with some of the neighbors. They had a terrible fight sometime on that trip. On the airplane home, they sat separately. When they returned home, my father moved downstairs. He became aggressive toward her, and I remember a time he started throwing dishes and cups in the kitchen. She was a mess. She'd often cry. We had a live-in housekeeper from Trinidad. It was her room that he moved into. Things were not comfortable for the poor woman, and one day, I remember seeing her packed up and waiting at the end of our circular driveway for a ride.

My mother insisted they see a therapist. My father was not in agreement, but somehow, she persuaded him. They went to a psychiatrist. After a few weeks, my father was not buying into this guy's advice. He abandoned the sessions. But we, the three kids, were asked to partake in her therapy. I'm not sure what my brothers' thoughts were on this, but I too thought he was weird, and I could not relate to what he was preaching. He tried to work with us on anger issues. Thinking back, I'm not sure I was angry, as I was more scared about the future. By this time my father had asked my mother for a divorce. He assured us kids that we had nothing to do with his decision and that he still loved us.

I was a sophomore in high school, and I was very involved in modern dance. I was part of the Nassau County Ballet Company, and I was invited to take dance classes at NYU on Saturday mornings. I had supportive friends and a boyfriend. So, my parents' problems were not at the forefront of my world. However, once the divorce started to proceed, I'd find my mother asleep in bed when I got home from school. The boys were hungry, and dinner was not ready. I would have to wake her up and get her into the shower. Sometimes she would just suggest what I should make for dinner. She seemed like a zombie. I later learned that her psychiatrist had prescribed methadone to help her through her depression. He became her guru, doing anything he said she'd do.

At this time, getting a divorce in New York State took up to two years and was quite an involved process. One thing Elaine knew she needed to get was a "get." It is a document in the Jewish court that ends a marriage. Once she got that, she decided to speed up the divorce process and took a trip to Mexico, where it was much easier to file and receive a divorce. This took about two weeks, and Elaine made it into a vacation, enjoying her time away. The divorce was finalized sometime in late 1969. For a while, things, although not perfect, were livable. Then, in 1970, Murray stopped paying alimony. Elaine was devastated. She tried suing him, but he ended up changing his name and moving out of state. I remember Elaine going door to door on Central Ave. looking for a job. A shop that sold all sorts of international items hired her. It was an import store, and I got to work there after school and on weekends. She wasn't making a whole lot as a salesclerk, and she found the owner to be gruff. So, Mike Weber, our next-door neighbor, came to her rescue. He was involved in renting spaces in the garment industry area of NYC. He got her a job working as a bookkeeper in a factory that made handbags. I drove her to the station in the morning, and she'd take the Long Island Railroad into

Manhattan. I would drive myself to school, and at around six, I'd pick her up. She lasted almost a year there. Her boss, Barry, was very nice, but the place was rat-infested, and she was lonely. All the workers spoke Spanish and had nothing to do with her. One good spot in her life at this time was when she started dating a man named Lou Morgan. He was extremely good to her. The problem was that he lived pretty far away from us in South River, New Jersey. The other problem was that he was not sophisticated enough for her. Lou really tried to make my mother happy. But she finally ended it.

I was away in college at this time, but my two brothers were still living at home, and they were both in high school. Somehow, Murray contacted her and apologized for all he did. He wanted her and the boys to move out to California, where he was living, and try to get back together.

As I said, I was away, so I'm not sure of the exact details, but he must have persuaded her because, in the fall of 1971, she, my brothers, and the dog all moved out to San Jose, California. They enrolled my brothers at Prospect High School in Cupertino. I came in and spent my winter break with them. The apartment he rented was beautiful, with a balcony that went along the entire outside and opened from every room. They were out there for almost six months. Elaine was not happy. She wasn't meeting anyone, and she missed her friends and family back in New York. Then an epiphany occurred to her. She discovered he had another woman in his life. By the end of February 1972, she packed up the boys and moved back home to Cedarhurst. It dawned on her that Murray was trying to get her to sell the house and give him the money. This she did share with me, and I applauded her for not falling into his trap.

When she got back to New York, Mike Weber helped her out again. He found a position for her in a more upscale building on 34th Street in

Manhattan. She worked as a manufacturer's representative. The company was called "Just Accessories," and it was conveniently located very close to Penn Station. So, after taking the Long Island Railroad into the city, she only had to walk a block to the building.

Elaine got friendly with the two other women who worked there. She liked meeting with clients from stores all across the country. She learned a lot about the wholesale and retail business, and this surely uplifted her spirits and excited her. Another thing she enjoyed was being able to dress up instead of wearing jeans and sweatshirts, which she wore at her prior job. Two partners ran the company: Sam Jackson and Richard Bloch. They both treated her professionally.

Richard Bloch, at the time, was going through his own divorce and confided in her about his whole ordeal. He probably felt she'd understand since she herself had gone through the same thing. In a matter of two months, they began a relationship.

Being away at school, I once again do not have many details about the early stages of their courtship. Steven, my middle brother, was in college at the University of Miami, and Rick was still in high school. I mention this because the one thing on Elaine's mind was how she was going to continue supporting the boys and paying for their college. I was lucky. When Murray stopped paying for my schooling, I immediately went to my financial aid office, and they set me up with an alumni scholarship and a small loan. I was given a work-study opportunity where I worked in the dorm's kitchen in the morning and at lunch, and in exchange, I got room and board free.

As soon as my youngest brother graduated from high school in 1975, she sold the house and moved into the city that summer. She found a one-bedroom apartment on Beekman Place, somewhere she had always dreamed of living. The apartment building even had a doorman.

After graduating from college, I came home and stayed with her in the apartment. I took a job in the garment industry since we had connections there. The apartment always felt odd to me, and it never felt like home. Richard Bloch was clearly present in her life. I remember that on Thanksgiving in 1975, my mother went to dinner at Richard's sister's home. She lived in a very prestigious building on the Upper East Side of Manhattan. When it was time to pick my mother up to go home, my brothers and I waited in the car for a while. My mother knew we were downstairs, and when she finally came down, she told us she mentioned we were there to both Richard and his sister, and neither one had the decency to invite us up. I would have thought that perhaps they'd want to meet Elaine's children since she and Richard had been dating for several months now. But I guess I was wrong. The feeling I got was that we were not up to their standards.

Another time, during the summer, I was walking down the street with both Elaine and Richard. He turned and looked at me disapprovingly and stated that I was dressed inappropriately. First of all, I'm not a person who wears low-cut tops or tight-fitting clothes. Apparently, the shorts I was wearing, which I believe were jean shorts, may have been too short or deemed informal to walk around in on the streets of New York City. I just kept my mouth shut, thinking all the while, who the hell is this guy telling me how to dress? I did not have a good feeling about him, and neither did my brothers. By early winter, I had decided to move back to Ohio to be with my friends. I rarely came home the rest of the year. I went back to school and started working on my master's.

Then, in the spring of 1977, Elaine informed me she was going to marry Richard. I was not happy and blatantly asked her why. Her response was, "I need to think of the boys." Was it an excuse? All I knew was that I didn't push the subject more or even try harder to talk her out of it. I could tell she had made up her mind. Elaine felt trapped, and she needed a way out. This guy was her ticket to a life without money problems. Nothing else weighed in. His arrogance attracted her, making him appear like a member of high society. I suppose this added to her ego because he chose her. They got married at her apartment on Beekman Place. His friend Buddy, a retired judge, presided over the event. Then they had everyone celebrate at the Park Lane Hotel, overlooking Central Park. She moved into his apartment at 400 East 56th Street.

Not wanting to cause a conflict at work, since she was now married to the boss, Elaine took a job selling carpets. When that got boring, she found another job with a furrier. Soon, the writing was on the wall. She preferred to stay at home.

After I got married and moved to Canton, Ohio, Elaine would often drive in and spend time with my family. She loved coming in and being with her grandchildren. But the drive from New York to Ohio and back was getting difficult. The winters in New York were also paying a toll on her, and she desperately wanted to move down to Florida. Many of her friends and family were already down there. It worked out well for her because Richard was asked to leave the company, and he ended up selling his half to his partner, Sam.

In 1993, Richard and Elaine built a beautiful home in one of the gated communities in Boca Raton. It had three bedrooms, an open kitchen, and a pool with a bonus room that was detached from the house. It was like a separate apartment, great for guests.

My family would often come down and stay with them for a week, during winter and spring breaks. My husband and I always stayed in the bonus room. My mother was so happy to have us visit. Richard, on the other hand, could not wait for us to go. He was uncomfortable with us being there, and he'd hide in a bedroom he made into his study.

We'd only see him when he came out for dinner. Going out for dinner with them was another ordeal. You can see the reluctance of Richard to pay the bill, and my husband would graciously cover it. Richard was never a good sport. Even with our children, you could sense his coldness. Certainly not the typical grandfather type. When we first arrived, he would greet my daughter and son with a small gift that you could tell he acquired from some free offer. He just didn't have it in him to be warm and loving.

There are some things I do know about Richard's background. He was born in Buffalo, New York. His parents moved around a lot. His mother was college-educated; she graduated from Cornell University. His father was not college-educated and worked his way up to managing large retail stores in several cities. One store in particular was Tiedtke's Department Store in Toledo, Ohio. The business was run by the Kobacker family, who also owned department stores in Boston and Columbus. Richard's father managed the Toledo store for several years until his death. But something happened there that involved Jerome Kobacker and Mimi Bloch, Richard's mother. Right after his father passed away, Mimi ended up marrying Jerome. My mother once told me that Richard felt Jerome was the blame for his father's poor health and heart attack.

Richard Bloch graduated from a prestigious high school called The Bronx High School of Science. Then he went on to complete his bachelor's degree at Emory University in Atlanta. He was smart and knew the right ways to rub elbows with the right people. Through business, he met many people who connected him to important sources. He was successful, materially speaking, but he lacked compassion. He married early in his career, which did not work out, and eventually had that marriage annulled. However, he learned many years later that he had a daughter.

The woman he had married, later became a college professor. She pretty much kept her daughter away from Richard. But when his daughter Hannah became an adult, she was curious about who her father was and contacted him. He was married to my mother at the time. Hannah Bloch is a successful international journalist. They ended up meeting in Florida and went out for dinner one time. That was it. She never had anything more to do with her father.

Richard went on to marry a second time. This marriage lasted for at least fifteen years. He had a son named Mitchell, with whom he kept up a relationship all his life. Mitchell's mother ended up marrying someone who moved the family to Beverly Hills. I remember hearing that Mitchell was going to Russia for his senior trip with Beverly Hills High School. My senior trip was to a park in Nassau County for the day. What a world of difference, I thought.

Once he and my mother were married, they traveled extensively. They attended the 1984 Summer Olympics in Los Angeles and traveled to Morocco, India, and China. My mother loved boasting about their trips and always said Prague was her favorite city. While in China, Richard began collecting Chinese figurines made of ivory. He referred to them as his Netsuke collection. Being an animal enthusiast, it infuriated me to see how hedonistically he glowed in showing his precious collection. He had a special enclosed glass shelf built on their wall once they got home. The pieces were kept enclosed with water in small cups to keep the ivory from drying up and to keep out atmospheric toxins. Becoming obsessed with his new hobby, he acquired several new ornaments to adorn his showcase. Each time we came down to visit, he had several new additions.

Then he began purchasing wall hangings from China. They were hung from a wall in the dining room. One spring break, when we came down and were having dinner, it happened to be Passover; Richard looked up and noticed one of his wall hangings was starting to fade. He began yelling at my mother about allowing the sun to shine in on those wall hangings. She was quite stunned and probably embarrassed. The next morning, I noticed he had covered them with big beach towels in the hopes of preserving the delicate prints.

I do need to mention that after Elaine and Murray divorced, her psoriasis cleared up miraculously. But one thing she could never have were pretty nails. Her nails were chewed up, and the areas surrounding her nails were puffed up from biting the cuticles. I attribute this to her being nervous. Was she living with a tyrant? Perhaps, or was he just the ultimate control freak?

Another incident that happened while we were there for a family vacation in Boca was when Elaine brought home a puppy. My mother loved dogs, as I said before. They kept her company, and she could love the dog, and in turn, it would love her back. One Saturday morning, we were going to Dick's Sporting Goods Store. Right next door was a PetSmart. In the parking lot in front of PetSmart, there was a fenced-in area with puppies up for adoption. My daughter grabbed my mother and guided her over to look at the puppies. My mother's desire was reawakened, but she was hesitant, knowing full well that Richard would not approve. My daughter looked into her grandmother's eyes and could see her yearning. With some coaxing and subtle begging, Elaine surrendered to her craving. She selected an all-white puppy that resembled a snowball. She envisioned this being a lap dog that would sit there and enjoy my mother's chebitzing. The pup came with a name, Bella, which means beautiful in Italian. We were told she was part Chow. My husband went into PetSmart and bought my mother all the items she would need to take care of the dog, including a cage. When we got back to her house, my husband and I started setting up the cage. Richard came into the room and kicked it down. He was apparently showing his disapproval. I looked over at my mother, and she said, "I don't care; I want something to love." He must have gotten used to it because he didn't give the dog away. He simply put up with it.

I would speak to my mother almost every day. After about a month, she informed me the dog was growing. Then the next month, she'd tell me Bella was getting really big. After about six months, she realized Bella was not going to be a lap dog. She loved her just the same. Bella was once again a true companion. Elaine would take her into the shower to wash her. Then I learned Bella was permitted to sleep in their bed. What a transformation. I think Richard finally saw that my mother needed to receive affection somehow since he was not offering it.

As the new century began and I hoped for a happier and brighter future, I only began to see my mother getting sadder. She even began to consider divorce. When I came in to see her, she had me take her to speak with a divorce attorney in Boca. I didn't go in with her, but when she came out, it appeared that the cost would be too high, and she knew Richard would never pay for it. The lawyer also made her realize she would lose everything, sending her into a life of destitution. So, she put that to rest.

Elaine had been a smoker all her life and finally quit sometime after marrying Richard. However, much of her lung capacity had decreased. By 2009, she was placed on a nebulizer and was required to use an oxygen machine to help open up the bronchial paths. She was eventually diagnosed with COPD.

One time when she came up to Ohio to stay with us for a while, she must have done some research because she wanted me to take her to check out a fifty-five and older community in Hudson, Ohio. She had read how wonderful this facility was, and it was close to where we were living. My guess was that she was planning another way to get out of being with Richard, just pick up and move away. We drove over there, and it was truly a beautiful place. We took a tour and met with the manager. I was willing at this point to help her out financially, but the manager told her she would not be accepted there because of her need to be on oxygen. Another door closed. Reluctantly she returned home. But my mother made regular trips up to stay with us during the summer months.

One of my most memorable occasions was taking walks with her on the trails of Cuyahoga National Park, near our home. She loved to see the frogs lying on water lilies in the pond and watching the herons as they created their nests high up in the trees. She found it to be not only remarkable but also exciting. I loved seeing her happy. One time she even said, pointing to a mobile home site right by the park, "That's where I want to live; I'll get a mobile home; I'll be close by." I would have loved that, but she was still married, and she knew how hard the winters would be.

When she did stay with us, she enjoyed cheering on my son during his baseball games and going down to Columbus to visit our daughter at Ohio State. She truly took pride in her grandchildren, whom she loved dearly. Elaine was always present for important family events like graduation, bar and bat mitzvahs, our daughter's baby naming, our son's Bris, and being there during my hospitalizations at the Cleveland Clinic when I had a partial colectomy. Richard did come up with her for most of these milestones. When he did accompany her, he didn't like staying at our house, and he and Elaine would stay at a hotel nearby.

Then, in April of 2010, Elaine had her first big fall. She was 79. I was up north, and she described how she fell in her home in Florida. She got up from sitting by the computer to get something. When she came back to sit down again, the chair rolled away. Elaine was on the floor and could not move for a while. She crawled to the phone to get help. Richard was not home at the time. She was taken to the hospital and checked out. Thank goodness she hadn't broken anything. Her back was just badly bruised. This seemed to have debilitated her. By June, she was able to get around.

A month later, Elaine called me and said she wanted me to help move her up north to live with me. She had had enough of living with Richard. I had plenty of room. I even had a guest room downstairs next to a bathroom. She would only have to climb the stairs to shower, and I would help her with that.

So, in July of 2010, my daughter and I flew down to Florida. We stayed at a hotel while my mother was preparing her things and packing up. I think she told Richard we were taking her on a vacation because he let her use the car he got her to drive up to Ohio. She even took Bella and all of Bella's things. I did the driving. It took us two days to get from Boca Raton, Florida, to Akron, Ohio. We spent one night in a motel in North Carolina with the dog. Bella was nervous, and every time a person walked by our motel room, she would bark. It made my daughter and me crazy. But Elaine was finally able to calm Bella down, and we got some hours of sleep.

The first week up in Akron was great. Mom was in a very good mood, and she and Bella would take walks. Her back was finally getting better, and she was excited that she could walk all the way to the top of our street and back. That would be just a little under a mile.

Then a catastrophe struck. It was dinner time, and I was preparing something in the kitchen. I'm not sure how I was standing, but Elaine walked behind me and tripped over my foot. She lost her balance and landed on the floor in excruciating pain. I helped her up and slowly led her to her bed in the back room. I had her lie down and brought her Tylenol. It seemed to ease the pain, and she was able to sleep for a while.

The next morning, she was in really bad pain. I had to take her to the hospital. She was admitted to Marymount Hospital in Garfield Heights, Ohio. After two days there, she demanded I arrange for her to be taken out of there and taken up to the main campus of the Cleveland Clinic, which I did. Elaine was much happier there. The doctor assigned to her care told me she would have to go into a nursing home to rehabilitate. I went home, and the next day, I checked out several in my area until I found one that had availability. It wasn't far from my home, and it was actually very nice.

After a week in the hospital, an ambulance transported her to the nursing home I had arranged for her. There she had her own private room, and she had physical therapy every day.

Elaine's mood had drastically declined. She seemed defeated and very angry. She would tell her friends and family on the phone that she came up to Ohio, and her daughter put her in a nursing home. I could not believe what I was hearing. She neglected to tell them she had an accident, was taken to the hospital, and was now in a rehab facility. But that was my mother lashing out.

During her stay there, she had a team working with her. Besides the nurses and physical therapists, there was also a social worker. As the team was getting close to discharging her, they called for a meeting that included Richard by phone conferencing and myself. The team went over what they prescribed for Elaine. That included the new medications she would now be on and reviewing those she had been taking. Was I surprised that Richard was included? I think I was, but looking back, she must have told them she was married, and obviously her care was covered by the insurance that Richard provided.

Finally, after six weeks of rehabbing, I was able to take her home. It was the end of August, and the weather was hot. She and the dog took short walks in my neighborhood. One of the things she insisted on doing was taking the sterling silver flatware she had brought up from Florida and pawning it. It had been Richard's mother's set from when his mother was married to Richard's father. All the pieces had the letter B on them. My mother hated it and was anxious to get rid of it. We drove to a shop in South Akron, and she received $3000 for it. Elaine planned to use the money for hearing aids she felt she needed and didn't think Richard would pay for.

A few days later, Richard unexpectedly showed up at my door. He had flown up and come to drive my mother and Bella back home. He did stay over one night, and the next morning he helped pack her up, and by the afternoon, she got into the car, and they drove away. My feelings were undeniably crushed. I had all the intentions of saving my mother, but I wasn't going to fight him. I had no legal right. He was still her husband, and unless she took legal action, there was not a thing I could do. The one problem Elaine faced all her life was relying on others to do her dirty work. She needed to face up to the downside of being single again, but she was too scared and would not stand up to him. So before long, she was back in Florida.

Things never got any better for her. Throughout the year she had problems breathing and needed to go to the emergency room to get her bronchial tubes opened. Then, in early spring of 2011, Richard decided they needed to move into an assisted living apartment. He put the house up for sale, and it didn't take long for it to sell. Before moving, I came down and helped her go through her things in her closets. There were things she was taking, things she wanted me to have, and things we were giving away. I boxed up my items and had them shipped up north.

By June of that year, they were in the new assisted living facility. Elaine would never have to make a meal; all that was provided. They luckily got a first-floor apartment with a small patio. This was so they could let Bella out, who was very good and trained to come right back in. During our winter break, we came down to see her. We stayed in a hotel and would come and spend time with her that whole week.

By this time, being as frail as she was, she had a healthcare provider named Marlene who came every day to help her get around. Where was Richard, you might ask? He was either at the Boca Raton Country Club having tea or closed up in his study on the computer. Richard's frugality was getting out of control. He would often question Elaine about what she spent or bought herself. Marlene would overhear his harshness toward my mother. This would upset Marlene, who was very worried and concerned for my mother's safety. She felt Richard was verbally abusive, and she thought Elaine needed to get out of the house. I received a phone call from Marlene and I had her put my mother on the phone. I spoke to my mother, and she said she would go somewhere. I remember this conversation because I was in my car, ready to go food shopping, and I spent the next hour locating a shelter for my mother in the Palm Beach County area. I finally found a place. Once again, I was planning on paying for this. It was a private home that opened its doors to help women dealing with domestic abuse. I set everything up and called Marlene back with the information. Then I finally went in to do my grocery shopping.

When I got back into my car, I received a call from Marlene, who said Elaine refused to go. That was it for me. I was tired. I had no more energy for her. I had my own home and family. This burden cannot fall on me any longer, I decided.

The first week of June 2012, I was still teaching. It was a Monday, and the last day of school was Friday. My brother Rick called me and told me Mom was in hospice. I couldn't believe it. I was irate. Richard went over me and called my younger brother. I happened to have been given her power of attorney in her health care, which we set up when she was at the Cleveland Clinic. I immediately called Richard and said I wanted her out of there and to place her in a hospital to help with her breathing.

He did have Elaine removed, and she spent one day in the hospital but fell out of bed when she tried to get up to use the bathroom. The next day her doctor personally called me and chewed me out for doing such a terrible thing and not following his orders, which were for her to be taken to a hospice facility. He claimed that prolonging her life was undignified and unfair. So that evening she was taken back to Hospice by the Sea. I flew out on Thursday after saying goodbye to my students and closing up my classroom.

Richard picked me up at Fort Lauderdale International Airport. I hardly said much to him the whole way to the hospice. When I got there, Elaine seemed responsive but very weak. She was hardly eating, and she was highly sedated for the pain. My middle brother, Steven, was also there. He actually lived in Boca Raton. Because he was working, he could only be there in the evenings.

I stayed at their apartment. Every day I drove over to see her. Each day she declined. By the end of the first week, she had no energy to talk. She'd use her eyes and hands to communicate. I fed her vanilla ice cream, knowing that was her favorite flavor. That's all she could eat. My brother told me she had whispered in his ear that she could feel herself shutting down. What a strange sensation that must be, I thought. She did have visitors stop in to see her. Her cousin Louis lived nearby, and her niece Dayle came in from Tampa. My younger brother, Rick, flew in and stayed for a few days.

After five days, I needed to get back home to help my son, who was starting an internship. I left on June 12th. My brother Steven called me Sunday morning, June 17th, to tell me Mom had passed away.

Prior to her death, Elaine requested two things. She asked me not to invite Carl to her funeral, and the other thing was to get a plot near where her parents were buried, at Mount Hebron Cemetery, in Queens, New York. Richard had a family plot in a cemetery at Mount Lebanon, but Elaine refused to be buried by him. This was clearly a final statement to Richard: "I don't want to be buried by you and be there through eternity." Rick went to the cemetery and found a plot at Mount Hebron. It wasn't right next to her parents, but it was in the same area. She was pleased with that.

Richard had her body flown up to New York and arranged for her to have a graveside funeral. He did not come up with her. He had a memorial service down in Florida for some of their friends. One thing I did not follow through with was not inviting Carl to her funeral. I could not grant her that wish. I invited him and his family. I did not do it out of disrespect; I did it out of practicality. She blamed him all those years, and I felt that was not reasonable. Besides, funerals are for the living. To me, Carl was her family.

What I felt most sorry about was her inability to do what she wanted for herself. She never appeared independent. Also, she lived through her children and their accomplishments instead of living life for herself.

MEETING JESUS IN HEAVEN

I recently had an image of myself dying and going up to heaven. It may have been a dream; I can't recall exactly. There at the pearly gates (and these were ornate wrought iron gates) stood a man. He was clothed in what appeared to be a white cotton robe with a string tied around his waist. The man, who seemed to be in his thirties, had long, disheveled brown hair and a beard. It dawned on me; he resembled pictures I had seen of Jesus. Then I thought, he's not letting me in.

Where did this idea come from, you might ask? I had been told, because I am Jewish, that I was a heathen and would not go to heaven. Who would dare say such a thing? Believe it or not, it was a principal I had worked under when we were living in Canton, Ohio. He tried everything to make me feel like an outcast and dropped hints that I needed to be saved. In other words, he was on a mission to convert me. In his mind, I would not go to heaven otherwise. That was back in the mid-1980s. If I knew then what I know now, I could have sued his sorry ass. But of course, not wanting to make waves and being new on the staff, I just let it roll right off. But now I realize subconsciously that I had buried that negative energy he was throwing at me. I'm glad the image came to me now so I can explore my feelings of being a victim of discrimination.

I grew up in New York, in predominately Jewish neighborhoods. My schools had many Jewish students. Growing up, I never experienced the feeling of being different or being a minority.

I went to college in Toledo, Ohio. That would be my first large encounter with students who were not Jewish. However, the funny thing was, that by my second day in the dorm, I was able to align myself with a group of Jewish students who were all living in the dorm. It was a coed dorm, so I mingled with both boys and girls who were the same as me. One girl was from Buffalo, one from Cleveland, and one girl was from Canton, Ohio. The boys were from New York, New Jersey, and Baltimore. We hung around together, and that made life at college more comfortable.

My first roommate, Nancy, was a gentile girl from a very small community west of Toledo called Defiance. I think at first she was a little fearful of me, but she finally relaxed, and we got along fine. She had a boyfriend who was attending another school but would come up on weekends. Sadly, during our first semester, she got pregnant. The only place to get a legal abortion back in the 1970s was in New York. She arranged to have the abortion at a clinic in Manhattan. So, I drove her to New York, and she stayed over at my home on Long Island. The next day a friend of mine drove us into the city, and we waited for her to have the procedure. She spent a few days at my home recuperating. Then we drove back to school. For a naive small-town girl to have to go through all that must have been very scary. But one thing is for sure, she got to see a Jewish person (probably her first) take good care of her. Unfortunately, she left school after that semester.

My next roommate was a Baptist girl from Pennsylvania. She was actually interested in learning more about my faith. She was very sweet and warm. She belonged to a sorority and often included me in some of the events. One time, she talked me into going to church with her. Being somewhat curious, I accepted. It was really foreign to me, but I was glad I went because it helped me understand where she was coming from. We got along well and respected one another.

Although I was in a city with a low number of Jews, I never felt out of place. The city had three synagogues and a thriving JCC. I met my good friend Linda Berg, who I still stay in touch with, at a University of Toledo baseball game. Someone introduced us. She was a Toledo native. We would go to a coffee house on Friday nights to listen to music. There, she introduced me to friends she knew from high school. We started hanging around with a group of her friends who knew other people who were either visiting from other schools or were studying law at TU. Eventually, this guy started coming around to the coffee house. It was now summer, and he was on break from medical school in Guadalajara. It wasn't until the following year that I saw him at the JCC, and we started dating. We married a year later. After living one year in Mexico and a year on Staten Island, we moved to Canton, Ohio, where he started his residency. This was a different world for me.

After applying to several school districts in the area, I was offered a position as an auxiliary teacher hired by the public school to work in a parochial school located in the district. I was to teach the gifted reading program. It was a great job, and I enjoyed my fellow colleagues. The first teacher I met, who worked with me in the trailer, asked me what church I belonged to. When I told her I was Jewish, her eyes lit up. I think that took her by surprise. But we got along fine and became very close. Luckily, a speech teacher was hired who also worked in the trailer, and she happened to be Jewish too, so I was not alone. Things worked out well for two years. I got along with the nun, who was a principal, but she and the priest had an affair and had to go. So, a new principal came in, also a nun, and when she learned I was Jewish, she decided to end the program. The district superintendent offered me a position at a middle school teaching remedial reading to seventh and eighth graders. That's when I had a principal who thought I was a heathen. The other teachers on staff were also cold toward me. Once in the teacher's lounge, I mentioned I was Jewish, and another teacher, who I got along with, said to me, "Oh, you are one of those." I immediately asked what he meant by that, but the assistant principal, who was there, quickly intervened. If I ever felt discriminated against, it was during my years working at that school. I was later assigned to another building, and that principal was even more prejudiced. He made my life miserable. I didn't have a classroom, so he had me teach in the hallway. One day I asked a third-grade teacher if he would let me use his classroom during his prep time, and he said no. Maybe I shouldn't have taken it personally, but I felt very alienated from the entire staff at that building. When I requested time off for my holidays, the school's secretary made a fuss about it. I always used my personal days, so I don't know why it would have been an issue. Once again, I saw that she didn't care for Jews. The last straw was when the principal there accused me of laying my hands on a student, which I knew I didn't do. I knew it was time to make a change. I ended up taking a job up in Cleveland at a Jewish day school, teaching a sixth-grade secular class in the afternoon and acting as the special education coordinator in the morning. The job was fine, but the drive there and back to Canton was grueling. However, I took my children, along with a few others, to the school. This was the first time I had to deal with very controlling parents who felt they were privileged. I didn't care for the environment. So, I decided to go back to public school teaching, which was my best move ever.

 At this time, we had moved up to Akron. I applied for positions all around the Akron area. I was offered a part-time position in the morning at a district in Peninsula, Ohio, called Woodridge, and at the same time, I got an afternoon position at my local district in Copley at a school called Arrowhead. It was fine. I didn't mind the commute between schools. I basically ate my lunch in the car. Eventually, the following year, Woodridge offered me a full-time position in their intermediate building. It was my very favorite position. The staff was wonderful and very accepting of me. I retired from that district after working fifteen years there.

Getting back to the image I had, I'm still not sure if it was in a dream or just an image that popped into my head while I was out walking. In either case, I knew I was not allowed in. In retrospect, if I were standing there with Jesus in front of me, I would probably have a lot to say to him. I'd tell him about all the trouble he has caused in the world. All the wars started because of his teachings. The need for countries to conquer other lands in the name of Christianity during the Crusades, with the aim of converting all those they conquered, or how Spain exiled Jews who would not convert to Catholicism or the pogroms across Russia. Six million Jews were killed because they were different, and there were other genocides and massacres of all those who were not Christians. I would let him know that he is behind the Christian extremist views that feel the need to purify the world with their Christian values. The whole idea of being saved is over my head. What are we being saved from? If it's going to hell, that concept is not part of my upbringing.

Now in America, where I live, I have to fear for my life again. Synagogues are the target of violence. White supremacists are going into synagogues and shooting congregants.

Even today I heard a podcast about how democracy is being threatened because we are now faced with a group that identifies themselves as Christian Nationalists. They want to make sure their Christian values are at the root of our government. These people seek to pass laws that reflect their views in political and social life. They've identified seven spheres they wish to have a hand in.

This includes arts and celebrations, commerce, education, family, government, media, and religion. If they gain power, minorities who are not practicing Christians are in trouble. I heard one politician, who identified herself as a Christian Nationalist say, "America was founded by white Christians and should remain this way." How scary it is to learn that this rhetoric is being chanted and gaining support. I truly think that if Jesus saw what was going on in America today, he would be appalled. For someone who preached love thy neighbor and seemed full of compassion, he would be turning over in his grave.

It's too bad; I probably won't meet him in heaven, nor will I meet him on earth. I was taught that Jesus was a rabbi with innovative ideas that didn't go over well with the rabbinical council at the time. He was deemed a troublemaker who was trying to change things regarding Jewish traditions. So unfortunately, he, along with two thieves, were placed on the cross to die. People who followed his teachings were ready for a change. That's why he became so popular.

Now for a brighter side to this issue. I once had a principal at Woodridge who personally came to me with a problem. Knowing I was Jewish, he asked me how I would handle the situation. Two boys were fighting over a piece of equipment; it may have been a ball or some other item, I can't remember. I told him I would do what King Solomon did when the two women claimed the child as their own. "When you tell the boys you will cut it in half equally, give it to the one who walks away from it first." Another time, while teaching at the middle school in Canton, the students always asked why I was absent the day before. So, I told them I had a religious holiday. They were perplexed, so I mentioned

I was Jewish. A boy in the front row immediately called out, "You killed Christ." I looked him straight in the eye and said, "I'd never kill anyone or anything. I have your best interest at heart, and you have no reason to fear me." He smiled and settled down.

Finally, just this school year (2022), I was substituting at a high school in Indio, California. The school is predominately made up of Hispanic students, a few white and black kids, and a handful of Muslim students. As one class was entering the room, I heard a student call out to another student across the room, "You Jewed me." After taking attendance and getting everyone into the lesson, I invited the student up to my desk and quietly explained, "You are not in any trouble, but I heard you say a derogatory statement when you came in earlier; you told another student he Jewed you. I am Jewish, and that hurts my feelings. It's a term that is racist and full of hate. I would appreciate it if you would refrain from ever saying it again. I understand you may not have known I was Jewish and didn't intentionally try to hurt me; I just want you to know we need to be kind in this world and language such as that will only spread more hate." He apologized and felt bad, but he seemed to get the message, and for that, I'm thankful.

So, in conclusion, I think I would tell Jesus, if I actually had the chance, that it is time for him to come down to earth and tell the people the truth. He needs to make things right. I'm tired of looking over my shoulders when I'm out of my comfort zone. I don't want to feel the fear of expressing who I am and what I believe. Most of all, I want my children and my children's children to feel free to be proud of who they are.

MASTECTOMY

I grew up with all-girl cousins. Two were older than me, and they were my role models. The one who was three years older than me was way cooler than anyone I knew. I observed her every move very carefully.

By age twelve, I had not gotten my period yet. I heard the girls at school talk about it. The big thing was that some of the girls were wearing bras. I would check myself out in the mirror. All I had were buds for breasts. I spoke to my older cousins about this issue, and they told me about training bras. With that information, I went running to my mother, demanding I needed to get a training bra.

We went shopping. The lady at the store pulled out several boxes of Playtex bras to try on. Although they were simply like ace bandages, I wanted one. Going to school the next day, wearing that bra, made me feel so grown up.

It wasn't much longer when I realized I would need something with cups. Before I knew it that year, I went from a 34AA to a 34A. At the end of my 13th year, I started my period, and I was officially a 34B.

Looking back at that time seems so comical. I'm sure most girls probably did the same hand-cupping routine in front of the mirror every day until, finally, the day came when their hands grabbed onto something substantial.

Then, as the years went by, I didn't give my breasts much thought. I never had cleavage, but that didn't bother me. When I got pregnant with my first child, I knew I wanted to nurse. I heard how much better it was for the baby than formula. But a strange thing happened in the last trimester. I felt a lump on my right breast. I went to see a doctor in my small town who told me I'd have to dry up after delivery in order to have a biopsy. I was determined to breastfeed my baby, so this was not an option. My husband helped me locate a doctor who would perform a biopsy without me having to give up nursing. We found a breast surgeon in Cleveland. Five days after delivering my daughter, I went up to Cleveland totally engorged and had the biopsy. I remember how painful it was. But the good news was that, even though he extracted a tumor the size of a walnut, it was not cancerous. I was able to breathe a sigh of relief.

Three years after that, I was diagnosed with Crohn's disease. I was put on a high regiment of prednisone to manage it. Not long after, my gastroenterologist, whom I liked very much, retired. I went through several of his partners who, for some reason or another, also left the area. Finally, I began seeing a doctor who was considered innovative. He put me on several different medications. All of these medications were biologics, which suppress the immune system. The one I was on the longest and seemed to have the best results was Remicade. Unfortunately, after several years, I developed an allergic reaction. So, the next medication I was prescribed was Humira. I was on all these drugs for over ten years (1990–2012).

Then, in June 2012, the day after returning from being with my mother in hospice, I found a lump on my left breast. That was on a

Wednesday. I was able to get into a breast specialist at an affiliated hospital of the Cleveland Clinic on Friday. I had an MRI and an ultrasound, and then the surgeon biopsied it. I went home and had to wait for the results after the weekend. Meanwhile, on that Sunday, my mother had passed away. On Monday, the doctor called and told me I had breast cancer. I was numb. Both my children were home, and I had to break the news to them right after learning their beloved grandmother had died. We all just cried for a while. Then I had to say, "We're strong; we'll get through this."

That week, my husband and I met with the breast surgeon. The tumor was five and a half centimeters. So, the first thing she wanted to do was try and shrink it using a round of chemotherapy. The hope was to possibly have a lumpectomy. An oncologist was added to my care who placed the order for Doxorubicin, also referred to as the Red Devil, because of its distinct red hue and fearsome toxicity.

Prior to starting the chemo, I had to do two things. First, I had to have a port surgically placed under my skin on my chest. This was so the nurses could easily get the injection directly into the bloodstream without always using my arm. The next thing I had to do was cut off all my hair. I was told by others who'd been through this how scary it was to wake up and find your hair falling out on your pillow. I didn't want to find out what that was like. Once my hair was buzzed off, I looked into getting wigs. I ended up with three different wigs. They were actually very nice looking.

Then, in early July, I started chemotherapy. I went to Medina Hospital, which was closer to my home, rather than driving all the way up to the main campus of the Cleveland Clinic. I usually had the chemo done on a Wednesday, and then I'd skip a week. But the week after receiving chemo, it was necessary for me to go back and get an injection of Neulasta to help build back my white blood cells. The whole round of this regiment lasted until the end of August. At the beginning of September, I had another MRI to see if the tumor had shrunk. Unfortunately, it did not. Therefore, the consensus was that I would have to have a mastectomy. As upset as I was, I remember thinking, I just want this thing out of me.

The surgery was set for September 25th, which was Yom Kippur. I thought about changing the date, but my husband insisted I just get it done. "Your health is more important," he reminded me. I went to see a plastic surgeon to find out if I would be able to have an implant placed inside where the breast tissue would be removed. He carefully examined me, looking at all possible places to use fat from my body, but there simply was not enough, so I was not a candidate for an implant. Another door closed.

I'm married to a very special man. I never doubted his love, and at this time, we had been married for thirty-four years. I mention this because, going through something like this, you can't help but think about your physical appearance and how unattractive you might feel. But luckily, I never felt he was put off, and he always continued to show me affection.

The surgery went well. I had to stay in the hospital for about three days. Besides being bandaged up, I had drainage tubes coming out of my side. Apparently, I needed to have five lymph nodes removed because they showed signs of cancer cells.

At this time, I was in my 34th year of teaching. Fortunately, I accumulated enough sick days. Friends and colleagues from school would stop by and bring us meals and vegetables from their gardens, and I even received a mug signed by all the teachers wishing me a speedy recovery. They kept me in the loop about all that was going on at school.

In November I started another round of chemo. This was for the whole body. The purpose of this round was to make sure any cancerous cells that may have traveled through my body would get destroyed. Again, the regiment was every other week, with Neulasta as the white cell builder in between.

All through my ordeal, I always had someone come and sit with me while I sat in the chair, taking in the cocktail that usually lasted two hours. I was so tired afterward; it was good to have someone drive me home. It was also tough eating. I lost my appetite, and I really had to push myself to eat. One friend suggested looking into comfort foods like macaroni and cheese, eggs, grilled cheese sandwiches, and peanut butter sandwiches. I also liked chicken soup and made sure I drank plenty of fluids.

Finally, after the last week of chemotherapy, I went to see the breast surgeon for a follow-up. She gave me a prescription for a prosthesis and also addresses of places where I could get fitted for special bras. She also wanted me to have radiation, which I did between January and February of 2013. I was back to work, so I went for the radiation very early in the morning and got to school in time to teach.

The prosthesis worked out well, but soon I learned I had to put it in other things besides the bra, like certain tops and bathing suits. Life as I knew it would now be very different. I had to be aware of buying clothes, particularly tops that were not too low and covered my chest area. Also, tops had to have high backs, in other words, no spaghetti straps, no low cutbacks on dresses, and no dresses with off-the-shoulder tops. It's amazing how my wardrobe changed.

But perhaps the hardest part of all this was how modest I would have to be around my husband. I no longer felt free to undress in front of him. I felt like I had a physical deformity and that it would surely not be very attractive. Intimacy was also affected. I'm thankful for having a loving and caring husband who would never want me to feel ashamed of myself. He has always made me feel respected, but I knew in the back of my mind that his approaches toward me needed to be more mindful.

The research says that every one out of eight women will be diagnosed with breast cancer. That's a high percentage. You have to wonder why so many of us are struck by this disease. Many times, it runs in the family. On my mother's side, there was no one who ever had it. On my father's side, his first cousin, Frances, died of breast cancer. My father was an only child, and his mother died of leukemia at age fifty-nine. So I asked my oncologist to test me for the BRACA gene. Having a daughter, I felt I needed, as well as she needed, to know.

I met with a genealogist, and after some questioning, she finally consented to having my blood drawn to see if I carried the gene. In the back of my mind, I thought perhaps my father could have been a carrier. But the test came back negative. So what could have caused me to suddenly develop breast cancer? I say suddenly because just eight months earlier, in October 2011, I had a mammogram and nothing suspicious was noted. Now, one has to rely on logical theories. As I mentioned earlier, because I have Crohn's disease, I was treated with medications that were immune suppressors. One thought was that by suppressing the immune system, you could allow damaging cells to get through the body's natural defense shield. It could have developed due to environmental factors. This would be hard to prove because I would not even know where to start, and no one I knew in my immediate community had been diagnosed with breast cancer. The biggest possibility for me was stress. I had been running back and forth to Florida dealing with my mother's declining health.

Getting through the last half year of 2012 was really traumatic. But I managed not to dwell on it while going through it. I kept my mind on other things, including reading a really long book, *Pillars of the Earth*. I still needed to be monitored. For the first five years after being diagnosed. I was required to have PET scans to make sure the cancer hadn't spread. I also needed and still have to have MRIs taken every year of the chest area and, of course, annual mammograms.

Has anything good come out of this experience? For sure, yes! I look at life differently. I have learned to let the little things go and to not get upset when things don't work out. I'm careful about choosing who I want to get close to. By that, I mean, I don't want to waste my time getting close to people who have close minds or are only into themselves. I also step back and analyze situations more carefully.

Having a mastectomy and dealing with cancer has made me see things in a more objective manner. I'm less judgmental and critical of others. I try to be more understanding, especially when people say hurtful things to me or to someone I love. I simply chuck it up to ignorance and let it go. There is certainly less confrontation; life is too short for that.

WHERE IS HOME

▷ ○ ☐ △ ▷

I was born in Brooklyn, New York, on June 2, 1953. Our first home was on Bergen Beach, probably the furthest east you can get in Brooklyn. When I was five and in the middle of kindergarten, my family moved to Far Rockaway, which was across the Marine Park Bridge in Queens. While there, I attended P.S. 215. I was finally getting settled in. Then the school began something called a split session, which meant the school day would be cut in half. At the time, my mother was helping my father out in his business and needed to find a better alternative. When I finished first grade, my parents enrolled my brother Steven and me in a Jewish day school called the Hebrew Institute of Long Island (HILI). When I began second grade, I was placed in a first-grade Hebrew class in the morning, and then I'd go to a secular second grade. I felt really strange there. It was a very strict orthodox school, and we were not orthodox. Even at lunch, I remember how they would check what we were eating. My mother was always careful and made sure it was not treif (unkosher). I made one good friend there, Ricki Fenster. Many years later I discovered she was going to the same junior high school as me.

HILI started early, at about 8:00 a.m., and went on till 4:00 p.m. That really helped my mother out with her work schedule. Then, when

I was about to start fifth grade, I was reenrolled back at P.S. 215. I had more friends there, and most lived in the projects (apartments) across the street from us. At this time, my mother wanted us to continue with our Hebrew studies. After school, two days a week, my brother Steven and I would walk to town and attend classes. I didn't like going there. It felt like a drag, and I was really turned off. But I guess my mother wanted us to be consecrated. As soon as that was over, I was done with Hebrew school. The one thing I remember about living in Far Rockaway was the summer. My mother had all three of us walk the two-mile trek from our house to the beach carrying all sorts of things like blankets, food coolers, or folded chairs. We schlepped all those things past the row of bungalows that lined the street to the beach entrance.

The following year, our family moved again. This time we moved to Cedarhurst, out on Long Island in Nassau County. This was the beginning of sixth grade. Like most girls at this age, I was self-conscious about how I looked and appeared to others. I immediately picked out the popular girls, who didn't seem to notice me. I befriended a girl named Allison, who was also new to the school that year. Her house was right across from the school. I spent a lot of time at her home. I remember she had lavender carpeting throughout her home, and her mother told me to call her Bunny. Sometime that year, I remember her father being arrested; he may have been involved with the mob. Luckily, she remained at our school. Then, when we began junior high school, I made new friends, and most were from around my neighborhood. We stayed in Cedarhurst throughout my high school years. Even though my family life was a mess, I managed to find many ways to stay busy and not let my parents' problems be my problem.

In my senior year of high school, I was determined not to stay in the New York area for college. I needed to cut ties with my mother, who had been getting used to relying on me. That year, several college recruiters would visit my high school. I would sign up to hear what their school had to offer. Some schools were too small or just didn't seem that exciting. The recruiter from the University of Toledo did catch my attention. When I went home and looked at a map, I figured it was far enough away and I'd still be able to get home in a one-day drive. I decided, what the heck? I'll just go there. So, after a summer trip to Israel with some friends, I came back and packed up to drive to Ohio with some other friends who were going to Cincinnati. From Cincinnati, I took a Greyhound bus up to Toledo and a taxi to the university.

It was mid-September 1971. Once I got to the campus, I got all unpacked in my dorm. The next day, which was a Monday, I went to the registrar's office and signed up for classes. Then, a few days later, classes started. Everything up to that point seemed to be going smoothly. However, the classes were going to be a challenge. I never had a syllabus before. Although I was familiar with due dates, these classes seemed to be demanding a lot of reading in such a short time. Then I had to deal with the bookstore and learn how to find books for each course. Getting through those first couple of weeks was quite an accomplishment for me. At the same time, I was meeting new people and partying. I was completely on my own, and I had to learn how to manage all these new experiences. I was ecstatic to have gotten through my first year without any incidents. As I mentioned, the remainder of my college expenses were totally on me, and I was very fortunate to have been offered a scholarship, work-study, and financial assistance. I grew up while I was in Toledo. When I graduated in June 1975 with my Bachelor of Education (B. Ed), I returned home to New York. Things were not the same. My mother had moved into the city. She sold the house in Cedarhurst right after my younger brother graduated from high school. I ended up working in the garment district in New York. I tried working for two wholesale businesses. I hated what I was doing. I wanted to teach, and I missed my friends back in Toledo. By September, I had made up my mind to go back to Toledo.

I was able to move in with friends, and I ended up substituting for a year. I also decided to go back to school and work on my master's. I got my first teaching job at the same school where I did my student teaching. The principal and I got along very well and helped me when I was doing my student teaching because my supervising teacher was never available to oversee me. He was the one who told me to get my reading certification and that he would hire me. So, I taught reading for two years at Washington Junior High School.

During my second year of teaching, I met my future husband. We got engaged on Halloween night in 1977. After getting married the following summer, we moved down to Guadalajara, Mexico, so he could complete his medical studies. We actually drove all the way down, stopping one night in Memphis and the next night in Monterrey, Mexico. This was such an adventure for me. I took in all the sights, and I was plastered to my window, not wanting to miss any of them. When we finally got into Guadalajara, I was so amazed at how beautiful the city was, with its splendorous flower beds lining the center of the boulevard as we drove. When we pulled up to the apartment we were renting, I was once again delighted to see a modern and clean building with an immense front glass window. I remember the street name was Calle de Mar. It was in a very nice neighborhood.

I knew I had better find something to do while Perry, my new husband, was in medical school. So I walked over to the American School of Guadalajara to see if they could use me in some capacity. I was pleasantly surprised that they offered me a teaching position right away. I taught English in the second grade during the morning, and then I had high school juniors who were preparing to apply to American colleges in the afternoon. I worked with them on writing, vocabulary, and language skills. I was happy there because I met many American spouses. We had a bowling league and a softball league. We found other American couples to go out with. We were only there for one year. Perry was given the opportunity to complete his last two semesters back in the United States. He chose a hospital that was located on Staten Island, New York. I was ok with that decision. I thought it would be nice to be back in New York and get to see my mother more often. My father and his new wife, Ruth, were also living in New York. I got to see them, and we would spend time in Glen Cove out on Long Island, where Ruth had a home. The funny thing about living on Staten Island was getting to take the ferry across New York Bay into Manhattan. Perry and I got to go to Chinatown and Little Italy quite often. Some Friday nights, we would go up to my mother's apartment for dinner.

The apartment we rented on Staten Island was very nice, except for the cockroaches that appeared in the kitchen from time to time. There was a great park right across the street from our building called Silver Lake Park. I would get up in the morning and jog around the lake. I did get a job on Wall Street, working for Oppenheimer. I worked as a secretary in the institution department. Each morning, I took the ferry over. Then a neighbor whom we befriended asked me to work for him at his firm. So, I moved up to Midtown and worked for him at Rothchild's. I still took the ferry over and then the subway to the office, but coming home, I discovered a bus that left right in front of Macy's and would drop me off at the corner of my street. Once again, we were only there for one year.

When Perry completed his medical training and graduated from the Universidad Autonoma de Guadalajara, he needed to complete a program called the fifth pathway in order to practice in the United States. We decided to return to Ohio. Case Western Reserve University offered this program in only two of its locations, Youngstown and Canton. Perry chose the Canton location and worked at the two major hospitals there, Aultman and Timken Mercy. We rented an apartment in North Canton. Interestingly, it was also located across from a great park called Price Park. Perry ended up doing his residency there and eventually took over a practice from an internal medicine physician who was moving to Michigan to pursue a fellowship in cardiology. I found a teaching position in the Plain Local School District. First, I was hired to work at a parochial school through auxiliary services to teach the gifted program, and then I was placed in the middle school and taught remedial reading. We ended up living eighteen years in Canton. I once had a cousin visit me. When we returned from shopping, she commented that she didn't see any black people. I realized, for the most part, that her observation was accurate. Although many African Americans are living in parts of Canton, the city does appear segregated and squeaky clean. It's quite provisional, sort of like Pleasantville. When we first moved there, most of the people we socialized with were from the medical community and those whom Perry worked with. When we began having our children, we joined a synagogue and the Canton JCC. Now we began socializing with people who had children the same age as ours. However, we remained more connected with the medical community. Then, in 1998, both Perry and I lost our fathers. His father, Ben, died in February of that year. Perry began to attend the Orthodox synagogue so he could recite kaddish for his father. We became very close with the young rabbi and his wife. We started to become regulars and stayed after services to learn more. As a result, we decided to become more frum and more orthodox. We still had to drive on Saturday because we were living on the other side of town from the little shul. Then a new rabbi came down from Akron, and he also filled a much-needed spiritual void we had. Eventually, we decided to send our children up to Cleveland to a Jewish day school. Luckily, I too, had the chance to teach at the same school.

By the following year, we had made a major move up to Akron. It would be easier for me to commute with the children up to Cleveland, and Perry could still drive down to Canton to his office. We purchased a very nice home in an area called Fairlawn. The neighborhood was great. We could now walk to the synagogue. Things were going well the first year. Then my daughter wanted to change schools. It was difficult for her to maintain friends from so far away. We enrolled her in another Jewish day school in Akron that was not orthodox but met her needs. She enjoyed that much more and made many new friends. My son, on the other hand, never had trouble finding friends. The new neighborhood had many more boys just around his age. He was never bored or lonely. We lived in Akron from 1999 to 2016. I found it to be a great place to raise our children. I found another teaching position not too far away. We had good friends there, and we enjoyed living in Akron. Perry even left his job in Canton and took a position with the Cleveland Clinic at a clinic in Independence, just south of downtown Cleveland.

When both children graduated from college, Perry and I decided to downsize. We put our home on the market in 2015. I retired from teaching the same year in February. We looked at several condominium communities. Unfortunately, the house was not selling. Finally, in the spring of 2016, we changed realtors. It was also about this time that Perry decided he needed a change. He wanted to leave the Cleveland Clinic. He felt the dynamics had changed there, and he described the environment as being toxic. By May the house was finally sold. We needed to get a place fast. After looking for several weeks, we found a condo in the Walden community in Aurora, Ohio. It was perfect. We moved there at the end of July. Also, after much consideration, Perry decided he wanted to live and practice in California. I felt he had to follow his dream. Our children were now adults and living their own lives, pursuing their own career paths. Perry worked with a recruiter who arranged an interview with a physician who had a private practice in Palm Desert.

We had spent a vacation in Palm Desert the year after my mother passed away. So, we knew the area and liked it. It had plenty of golf course communities that Perry would enjoy. We flew down there, and Perry met with the physician and his wife. He was offered a contract, but he didn't think the salary was high enough. As we were heading back to the airport in Los Angeles, a recruiter called Perry and told him about a practice with UCLA at a clinic they had in Santa Clarita. Since we were taking a late flight back to Ohio, we decided to check out that clinic. Perry was given an opportunity to speak with the program director over the phone, so I ended up driving most of the way from Palm Desert to Santa Clarita on Interstate 10 while he was having an interview. We got to the clinic around 4:00 p.m., and he met the other doctors who were practicing there. The practice was unique. This practice was set up to provide services to those who are part of the movie and entertainment industries. Predominately, the physicians there saw many people who were in the background of the movie industry, like grippers, makeup artists, seamstresses, etc. This was in the spring of 2016. Perry decided this sounded like something he wanted to do.

So, a few weeks later, we returned to Los Angeles, and he went through all of the HR procedures necessary to begin working up in Santa Clarita. We also spent that time looking for an apartment. Even though we were there for such a short time, we went out with my old friend Barry Laufman and his wife Helene, who live in the San Fernando Valley. We also got together with our friend Leslie Wilkof's brother Jeff and his wife at a restaurant up on a hill in Granada Hills. It was a lovely place, but I remember the food was not that great.

Then, in November, Perry moved to Santa Clarita. He was to start on December 1, 2016. I joined him on December 17th. While I was there, I decided to get a substitute permit. I drove to San Gabriel High School and took the CBEST, which is the California Basic Education Skills Test. It involved reading, math, and writing. Once I passed that, I applied for the subbing permit, and by February 2017, I started subbing in the schools. I found Santa Clarita to be a very laid-back town. It didn't have very much to offer. The only good thing it did have were great bike trails. Perry and I would go down to L.A. on the weekends. The restaurants were better there, and we often went to concerts there too. The problem with going down to L.A. from Santa Clarita was the traffic. It always seemed that no matter when you traveled on the highways, there would be traffic, even though they had six lanes. After subbing for five months, I felt I needed more to do. So, I applied and got my California teaching credential. I was hired in August to teach the English and health education courses at the L.A. County jail in Castaic, just up the road from us. This was a high school program called Five Keys that was first started in San Francisco. My students were all inmates who were working on receiving their high school diplomas. I never felt fearful because there were deputies all around. Also, the inmates I taught were trying to gain points for privileges. For the most part, they were respectful. Only once did I have to have a student removed for his continuing disruptive behavior.

On weekends, Perry and I would try to get out of Santa Clarita. One of our favorite places to drive to was Ventura County. He would find a golf course to play on, and I would locate a bike trail. There was also the outlet at Camarillo. I didn't mind living up in Santa Clarita, but after two years, Perry decided he wasn't practicing medicine the way he was meant to. The UCLA Medical System only allowed the physician fifteen minutes with each patient and thirty minutes for new patients. He felt rushed and not as effective as he should have been. At about that same time, a postcard came in the mail from the Eisenhower Medical Center recruiting internists for their semi-concierge program known as 365. Knowing the Palm Desert and surrounding areas, Perry immediately contacted the program director. Ironically the program director did her training at the Cleveland Clinic. We went down to Rancho Mirage, and he met with the other physicians who were part of the 365 program. Before I knew it, he had made up his mind to join them. While we were there, I met with a realtor who showed me several condominium communities. I didn't see anything I liked at that time, so we returned a few weeks later. There was a property we liked and started to go through all the purchasing arrangements, only to find we could not get a bank loan because this property was in a community that did not have a good reserve and there were many rentals in this particular development. So, we looked at some more until we found one we both thought was nice at The Lakes Country Club.

We moved down to our new condo in Palm Desert at the end of December 2018. We have been living here since. I go back to our condo in Aurora every summer when the temperatures in Palm Desert are above 110 degrees. We also go back to see our children in Ohio and New York for many special occasions like the births of our two granddaughters in Ohio and the bris of our grandson in New York. We try to get back to Ohio for birthdays and holidays. This year, our two children, along with their families, arranged a special 45th anniversary getaway for Perry and me in Woodstock, New York, the second week of July. They rented a house, and we all got to be together. My son had a photographer come up and take several pictures of us with the grandchildren, and then each family had pictures taken. It was a very memorable weekend.

I've lived in so many different places. I'm not sure we will stay in Palm Desert forever. I do think I will always return to Ohio. I can't say we will keep the condo in Aurora, but I feel I can always come back there and see my children, my friends, and all the familiar places I have enjoyed going to. They say home is where the heart is. Isn't Ohio the heart of it all?

THE WORST PAIN

The worst pain in the world is losing a child. Living each day after has to be like continuously having your heart ripped out. When you first bring a child into the world, as a parent, you start fantasizing about all the wonderful experiences this new being is going to have. Then suddenly a catastrophe occurs, whether by a terrible accident, a devastating illness, suicide, or murder. It even affects everyone in the family. No one is really ever prepared, and a feeling of helplessness continuously lingers.

The very first time I encountered grieving parents was when I was about eight years old. My family owned a two-family house in Far Rockaway, Queens. My parents rented the upstairs apartment to a couple and their sons. The mother was Helen, the father we called Hecky; it was probably Hershel, and their two sons, Billy and Jamie. Billy was about my age, and Jamie was two. I knew Jamie was disabled, but I didn't know what the problem was. Then one day, my mother came into my room and told me Jamie had died and that he had Tay-Sachs disease, which I later learned was a genetic disease primarily in Ashkenazi Jews. I remember how distraught Helen and Hecky were after that. Their son Billy, who I played with often, would now spend much of his time in his apartment. I also remember feeling sad for them. As an eight-year-old, this was a very new occurrence, especially since I had not experienced the death of a person before. They moved out of the apartment soon after.

While we lived in Canton, Ohio, one of Perry's colleagues lost his daughter to Hodgkin's disease. I knew the parents well because they were part of the Jewish community, and the father was also an internist. She was the oldest of four children. That same year, a couple who both practiced ophthalmology lost their son in an accident. He was attending Harvard, and while at a party, he fell off the balcony.

It's very difficult when you live in a small community and your children are growing up together. When we moved to Akron, we joined an Orthodox synagogue. As is custom, men and women sit separately. During a Yom Kippur service, a woman came in and began whispering to another woman beside her. Suddenly, I heard an agonizing gasp. I was sitting with two of my close friends, and we looked at each other with questioning expressions. Then we noticed other women, who were obviously told something, holding their faces in horror, and some began to cry. What could have happened to cause such emotions on the holiest of holy days? Before long the information was shared with the group of women I was with. We learned that one of our congregants' fifteen-year-old daughter had committed suicide that morning. What a shock I felt. I knew these parents and could not imagine what they could be going through. That week, I made a shiver call, and I realized, while standing at the front door, that I just didn't know what I could possibly say that would comfort them. When the mother opened the door to receive me, we simply hugged.

Sometime later, I learned that their daughter had been bullied at school. I'm sure if her parents had known this, they would have certainly done something to help and protect her from such cruelty.

When such tragedy strikes in your small community, everyone, and I mean everyone, gathers together. Not only is the family mourning, but we are all mourning. We questioned why, how this could happen, and what we could we have done to stop it. I watched each night of shiva, as one of my closest friends held a piece of her son's clothing to her face so she could still smell his presence.

It was June 2005. Jason was a college student living with friends in the house his parents kept in West Akron that had belonged to his grandparents. One night, after Jason returned home from playing music with his dad, he went upstairs to his bedroom and was getting ready for bed. His three roommates were downstairs playing cards. All of a sudden, the front door swung open, and two men stormed into the house, one holding a gun and asking for a particular person they claimed cheated them out of a drug deal. Evidently, the one they were looking for was playing cards, but he pointed toward the upstairs, indicating the one they were looking for was there. As the two men ascended the stairs, the three roommates scrambled out of the house in fear of their lives.

Jason heard the commotion and opened up his bedroom door. The man holding the gun shot Jason in the chest. Jason's parents were woken up by the police pounding on their door at five the next morning to deliver the worst news any parent would ever want to hear. That night changed so many people. This incident has stayed with me for a long time. Probably because we were so close to the family. Our children ran around with their two boys. Holidays and special celebrations were shared. All that summer, neighbors and friends banded together to help relieve the pain, knowing that when evening came and everyone left, there would be so much suffering. Some women came by and planted a garden in front of their house as a memorial. Others prepared meals. I took their younger son along wherever our son was going.

Summers came and went. People got back to doing their daily activities. We kept checking in on them. I would walk the path from my house through their backyard just to stop to chat. It was not surprising that the parents no longer wanted to be part of any social activities, including coming to synagogue during the high holy days. I can understand how hard it is to watch the other children in the community grow up, graduate from college, get married, and start a family. They say that time heals for those who go through the grieving process. I'm not so sure that applies to losing a child. Especially when there are things around you that remind you every day that the child you brought into the world is no longer there for you to watch grow into adulthood.

Why did I choose to write about this? The reason is that it never escaped me. When I look at my life, my family, and how fortunate I am, I also have to remember their pain. It grounds me and makes me realize that I should never take anything for granted.

A CONFLICTED SOUL

My father, Murray Antonoff, was born on January 24, 1928. He was the only child of immigrants Sam and Nora. They came to the United States from what was then the Russian Empire.

Nora Martin (whose name was changed at Ellis Island) came from Moscow. She grew up with five other siblings. Her father was in the czar's army, and they lived a comfortable life. When the Russian Revolution broke out in 1917, the family immediately left Russia. They went to Paris, France, and stayed there until they could get papers and enough money to pay for passage to the United States. After several months the family was able to leave. Her oldest sister stayed behind in Paris. She married and had two daughters. Nora and the rest of the family traveled to La Harve, France, and boarded a ship to New York. Like most refugees coming over, they settled somewhere on the Lower East Side of Manhattan.

I remember that Nora's sister Dora married and moved to Denver, Colorado. Another sister moved up to Ulster County in New York and started a dairy farm with her husband. Her younger brother, Albert, finished high school and graduated from college. He eventually taught Russian at the University of Michigan.

My grandfather, Sam, is a whole other story. He came from a small village near what is now Kiev. He grew up during the pogroms in Russia. These small peasant villages were the target of the rebel rousing Cossacks. They would storm into these small villages, looting and murdering young men. Luckily when a village was being raided, someone on horseback would escape the rampage and ride to the next town to give warning. Great-grandma Brauna had her three sons run to a nearby marsh that had a deep pond. They ducked under the water and used reeds to help them breathe. Meanwhile, when the Cossacks arrived, they rummaged through the house, taking whatever they wished, and even ripped the gold earrings right off great-grandma's ears. These kinds of incidents occurred for several years. Then, by 1917, when the revolution began, Great-grandma Brauna decided it was time to get her family out of Russia and move to America. She realized life would be intolerable as the communists came to power and further persecuted those who sought religious freedom.

So, Grandpa Sam, along with his mother, two brothers, and three sisters, found passage on a ship that eventually landed on Ellis Island. Here they met with immigration officials, and then doctors checked each family member over. Everyone was cleared to enter the United States except for Grandpa Sam. He was found to have an eye infection, trachoma, and was sent back on a boat bound for the port of Odessa in the Black Sea.

Once he arrived in Odessa, he stayed at the port and pretended he was a cargo handler. He loaded goods onto boats and unloaded cargo off boats. He hopped on a boat that was departing, unaware of where it was heading. Grandpa Sam discovered it was headed to Greece. At a port in Greece, he found another boat that would land in Italy. Finally, he located a cargo ship that was headed for the New York harbor. Pretending to be involved with the shipment, he pulled into the East Hudson River without having to stop at Ellis Island. He quickly disembarked and found his way to the Lower East Side of Manhattan. He looked for shops with Hebrew lettering to help locate his family. Knowing someone there could speak Yiddish and might have leads to where he could find them. He eventually tracked them down and was able to be reunited with his family. They were living in a cramped tenement house with another family.

Needing to work, Sam took a job sewing for a tailor. He did that for a few months, and then, using his sewing skills, he got a job repairing upholstery for the wealthy upper-class New Yorkers. After several years, he put enough money away to move his family to a house in Brooklyn and opened a shop repairing furniture.

I do not have fond memories of my father's parents. It was almost as if my brothers and I were forced to visit them. They were not very warm to us, and I felt that they weren't comfortable around us. Sam and Nora appeared to be bitter about having to be in America. I don't think they were prepared for what they would encounter once they got there. Life in America was foreign to them. They did not assimilate well. Mixing with other cultures in New York was very difficult.

The Lower East Side of New York was crowded with newcomers arriving from many countries. Besides the Jews from Eastern Europe, there were Italians and the Irish, all living alongside each other. Finding a job was hard. If you weren't a peddler, you were lucky to find a job in the sweatshops that existed and were willing to hire these desperate immigrants. The hours were long, and the conditions were horrible.

I have no idea how Sam and Nora met. I do know that they both belonged to an organization called the Workers Circle, which was later renamed the Workmen's Circle. The purpose of this organization was to promote social and economic justice in the Jewish community. It also provided education and year-round programs of concerts, lectures, and secular holiday celebrations.

Murray's parents could not let go of their opinions regarding how American culture was changing and how fearful they were of changing with it. An example that sticks out in my mind is when they came to babysit us while my parents were away on vacation. It was February 7, 1964, and the Beatles were performing on the Ed Sullivan Show. I had to beg them to let me watch it. In their minds, rock and roll was terrible, and pizza was poison. I put on such a stink about wanting to watch it that they finally gave in. I was so excited to see the Beatles and watch all the girls screaming in the audience. All the while I could hear Nora and Sam in the background grumbling about how awful the music was and listening to them mock the Fab Four.

Murray had a first cousin, Frances, who was Nora's niece. She was the daughter of Nora's oldest sister, who remained in Paris after the family moved to the U.S. When World War II broke out, the Germans entered Paris in 1940. Jews were no longer safe there. Frances's parents were shot on the street, and she and her sister survived by hiding at a neighbor's home. These neighbors were able to smuggle her out of France and send her to the U.S., where she was eventually able to reunite with Nora. Frances stayed with the Antonoffs for a short while. When she was old enough, she moved out, got a job, and married William Rosenbaum, who was also originally from France but got out before the occupation. They had three children: Phillip, Rachel, and Julie. Whenever my brothers and I went to visit Murray's parents, we would always hear how wonderful and cultured the Rosenbaum children were. All three of the Rosembaums played piano. I did take piano lessons, but I can honestly say that it was not my thing. I enjoyed learning to play the guitar more. But my real love was dance. However, we Antonoff kids were never good enough. The Rosenbaum children were perfect in Sam and Nora's eyes.

One thing I do remember about Nora is that she made delicious stuffed cabbage. She always served it when we came over. Nora passed away at the age of fifty-nine from leukemia. Sam remained in their apartment on Ocean Parkway in Brooklyn by himself for many years. He passed away in 1983.

Murray's upbringing was not easy. I believe he endured a lot of turmoil growing up. I had been told that when Nora and Sam would argue, Nora would take off with Murray for a few days or weeks until she cooled down. So, this must have played a large part in how he would later deal with situations that he could not handle.

Murray attended Erasmus High School for two years, then went to a vocational school to learn a trade. When he graduated, he enlisted in the Navy. WW II had ended, but he was sent to the Pacific Islands to ensure the Japanese had vacated all the bases, and his battalion searched through the jungles for any Japanese soldiers that were still there. While in Guam, he got dysentery. He was sent to a Naval hospital in San Francisco to recuperate. When he recovered, he stayed at the Naval Base in San Francisco for a while. Murray once told me he stole a Jeep for the day so he could get out and see the city. He ended up getting in trouble because he returned after curfew, and it was pretty late. He requested to be sent back to the Brooklyn Navy Yard to finish up his military duty.

Murray was not good at taking orders. He liked being in charge, and that made him a natural salesman. After he married Elaine and worked for his parents for several years, he started his own dinette furniture business with two other men. He was the salesman; one man took care of the books, and the other man dealt with the manufacturing end. This new company was called Antarenni, which took part of the last names of all three partners. The company did very well for many years. Then, sometime in the early '70s, wrought iron dinettes were no longer the trend. The company eventually disbanded.

As a salesman, he would go out of town to see customers and visit their showrooms. Murray at times had to spend several evenings away from home. Being young, I did not know what those sales trips involved. Now I am aware, and his infidelity and partying were later disclosed to me.

As a father, I found him to be attentive. He did punish me, and I remember once, after calling my brother a schmuck, he hit me with a belt. Ironically, it was a word he often used to describe someone he didn't like. But I also remember him taking me, and only me, out on special occasions. He took me for ice cream once because I gave my brother my ice cream cone when he dropped his. For my seventh birthday, my parents took me to Manhattan for dinner and to see the Rockettes at Radio City Hall. It was a special night with them without my brothers.

Then, in my senior year of high school because seniors ended earlier than the rest of the school, he took me to Chicago with him. It was the week of the American Furniture Mart. This is an important event in the furniture business, where many wholesalers and retailers come together. He was busy during the day, so I got to walk up and down Michigan Ave. looking at various stores. At night he got a young man to take me out on the town. First, we had dinner on top of the Hancock Building. It was the first time I had eaten at a place that revolved around. Then after dinner, he took me for drinks at the Playboy Club. I wasn't eighteen, but they never carded me. However, I did feel out of my element. I was suspicious as to why my father had this young man take me out instead of him. I later learned he was involved with a woman from Pittsburgh who was also attending the furniture mart.

Murray was protective of me. Another thing that happened during my senior year was going with him to visit college campuses. I had been accepted to Bard College, which is in Annadale-on-the-Hudson, New York. We drove up there one day in early spring. He saw some students smoking pot, throwing frisbees around, and what looked like a hippy hangout. It didn't take long for him to tell me to get back in the car and say, "You aren't going here."

I was never rebellious or disrespectful toward him. He did praise me once for a poem I had written right after Martin Luther King Jr. was assassinated. I remember that incident because he very seldom praised me. After my first year of college, he flew me out to California, where he was living. I stayed with him in his apartment in San Jose. I got a job at a store called GEMCO. Murray bought me a car that summer. It was a used Volvo 164 series. I loved that car. When I returned to Ohio, he drove it across the country for me. Murray wasn't making much money at this time. He tried starting a business that dealt with fish and aquariums. It just didn't take off. He stopped paying for me to go to college. Luckily, I was able to figure out how to handle that problem and was able to finish my four years with the help of financial aid and a scholarship.

While I was in California, I met Arleen. She and Murray had gotten married, but she eventually kicked him out, and their marriage ended in less than a year. Murray was not having very much luck making ends meet in California and realized he needed to go back to New York. He got himself situated in Middle Village, Queens. Once again, he tried getting back into making dinette sets. He even got my brothers involved. They found him difficult to work with, and he had limited resources. Knowing this was not going to work out, they both left him.

Murray's next venture was the flea market. He would go to several wholesale companies in the garment district of New York and buy up their seconds for very little money. These would be items that the company would not sell to retailers because they had small defects, like a tiny tear or stitching that was not exactly straight. He picked up ladies' jackets and coats. For a low price, he collected an inventory and would set up a spot at the flea markets, one weekend at Roosevelt Field and another weekend at Elizabethtown, New Jersey.

Sometimes, while he was living in Queens, he would frequent a singles bar on Queens Blvd. It was there that he met Ruth. She had recently been divorced and had three adult children. She fell head over heels for Murray. Ruth owned a home in Glen Cove, on Long Island. Murray ended up moving into her home. She and Murray together operated the flea market business. Ruth was Murray's right hand. Having now moved into a large home with a nice big garage was ideal for keeping their inventory. After a while, Ruth wanted a commitment. So, in the summer of 1979, Murray married Ruth. Perry and I attended the wedding, which took place at Ruth's home. I got to meet two of her children, Joan and Richard. Her oldest son, Barry, was a physician living in Arizona with his wife and two children.

Several years later, when Perry and I were living in Canton, Ohio, Murray came to visit us. He needed a new van. He researched and found a dealership near us that had exactly what he wanted. I ended up giving him $3000 for that van. The next day he drove back to New York.

Eventually, Ruth wanted to sell her home and move to Florida. They moved down to Turnberry, which was just north of Miami, in 1986. Once again, he needed to make a living and impressively got into estate sales. It was successful because when I came down to visit them, they ended up opening a shop selling merchandise from the estate sales.

Then, in the winter of 1994, Murray unexpectedly came to Ohio. He called me late one night and asked me to pick him up at the airport. I could not go up there, which was over an hour away, but instead I got my neighbor, Mark Kuntz, who was the eleven o'clock weatherman, to give him a ride home. I told my dad to take a taxi to the station in downtown Cleveland and that he would come back down to Canton with Mark. When he got to my home, he informed me he was leaving Ruth. He only stayed for a couple of days. The day after he left, Ruth appeared at my door. She came looking for him. I felt terrible for her. She stayed over one night and left. I don't know what happened right after that, but things must have gotten better because they were back together when my family came down to Florida over spring break. Although we would stay up in Boca Raton with my mother, he came up and took us down to Turnberry for a buffet dinner and to the place where he and Ruth were living.

Sometime in November of 1997, Murray called me to tell me he had been diagnosed with small-cell lung cancer. He had been a smoker most of his life. He stopped smoking three years earlier. I came down to see him in December. He had lost some weight, and he was already starting chemotherapy treatment. I remember him saying the hair on his face felt like needles. The unfortunate thing was, back in September, he went to the doctor for a persistent cough. That doctor simply prescribed cough medicine. It took two more months for his physician to recommend he have a chest X-ray, whereupon they found he had lung cancer. It had spread, and when I came back down to see him in August, he was so sick, he couldn't keep food down. He passed away at home on September 18, 1998.

As an adult child, I saw him for what he was. Murray was truly a conflicted soul. One thought about him was that he might have been bipolar, but he was never diagnosed. Thinking back, he did have mood swings. He also had to be right. It was important to him that people look up to him. Looking back at his childhood and being raised in what I consider a dysfunctional home, he developed low self-esteem. That, I believe, was the crux of the problem. Having low self-esteem caused him to have to prove how great he was. For the three of us, he seemed to want to look larger than life. A healthy parent tries to bring out the best in their children and guide them to success. I saw him compete with my brothers, put my mother down, and certainly not encourage me. Once I mentioned to him that I thought I'd study hospital administration, his comment was, "Girls don't go into that field; it's for men."

Another aspect of his low self-esteem was his womanizing. It obviously lifted his feeling of self-worth by winning over a woman. Interestingly, my brothers and I agree on the fact that he never had a male who was a good friend. Understandably, that would pose a threat. He must have suffered privately; I never saw him show remorse for his behavior.

In closing, however, I know how proud he was of me when I became a teacher. When he was out in Ohio, on one of his visits, he came and helped me set up my classroom. Also, he liked my husband and was honored when we asked him for advice about buying our first home. I'm sure he died knowing that all his children were self-sufficient, and that gave him peace of mind as he passed away.

THE ART OF TEACHING

When it came time to think about a profession, I knew teaching was my calling. I couldn't think of a more satisfying and rewarding profession than teaching. As in any line of work, there were good days and some challenging days. I was fortunate to teach in many different settings and at many different grade levels, along with some of the greatest coworkers. I grew with each year and with each new encounter. So, when it came time to retire, after thirty-seven years, I was satisfied that I had left my mark and could now move on. As one door closed, I knew I would be embarking on a host of new experiences. Someone once told me I would know when it was time to retire, and they were right. The old adage that you know when it's time is so true. I was exhausted, and now I wanted to satisfy my desire to travel.

When I first chose to go into teaching, I was planning on becoming a physical education teacher. In high school, I enjoyed all the individual sports like gymnastics, dance, and track. I also participated in the intramural volleyball games after school. I loved my health education class, so I thought I would major in physical education and minor in health education. When I got to college, during the first quarter, I had to take field hockey. I remember coming back from each class with bruises on my shins. The other girls were not quite like me. They seemed to be extremely competitive. Knowing I would be with this group going forward, I made up my mind to change my major. I switched to a major in school and public health with a minor in dance. I loved all my courses except for anatomy and physiology. But I managed to pass them both.

During my last quarter in college, I did my student teaching in health education at Washington Jr. High School. The cooperating teacher left me to teach reproductive health, which was my first teaching experience with a group of ninth graders. She took off and left me high and dry. I turned to the school principal for advice. I had him approve any videos I planned to show, and he recommended I send parents letters telling them what I planned to do and offer them the option of having their child participate or not participate. He also checked any diagrams I would be using in class. He pretty much monitored all my lessons for the whole nine weeks of my student teaching.

I was so thankful for his support and guidance that on my last day, I brought him a plant to show my appreciation. He told me the school was awarded state funding for a reading program and asked me how fast I could get the coursework done for a reading certification. Having no definite plans, I told him I could do it over the summer. He said he would hire me. So that is how I ended up becoming a reading teacher. While I taught at that school, I completed my Master's in Curriculum and Instruction over that year. I only taught there for two years because, after Perry and I got married, we had to leave for Guadalajara, Mexico, so he could complete his medical training. But the nice thing about working at that school was that I got to co-teach with a very wonderful woman, Dianne Carter, who taught me a lot.

In 1978, while Perry was attending medical school, I was fortunate to have gotten a teaching job at the American School of Guadalajara.

All the students were Mexican, but their parents wanted them to learn English. The school was certified by the Alabama state school system, and we followed their curriculum. When I was working with the junior English class, those who would be taking the SATs, I found the curriculum boring and often diverted by using poems and music lyrics to teach them English. The students seemed to be more responsive to that way of delivering the curriculum.

Then, in 1980, when we moved to Canton, Ohio, I applied to a few districts there and was hired by the Plain Local School System to teach at a parochial school in their district under auxiliary funding. The school was Our Lady of Peace, and I was to teach the gifted program. Teaching gifted students is a gift in and of itself. I was able to create lessons that I felt would challenge the students. My students could demonstrate that they attained the knowledge by selecting various methods that I gave them. For example, instead of writing out a book report, they could engage in a dialogue they felt was important to that book and tell why they chose it. Another option was to create a collage and discuss what the pictures represented in the story. Some did a makeshift video using a shoe box, and having pictures, they drew of the different scenes scrolled on an empty paper towel cylinder. It was very clever, and I was amazed at how they loved showing what they did. I was fortunate to have worked under an awesome principal, but she left after that year. Fortunately, I was able to complete my practicum under her for my elementary principal certification. I stayed at that school the following year. The new principal was not easy to work with, and I ended up teaching remedial reading. When she cut the program altogether, I was lucky the district placed me in the middle school, where I stayed for five years. I asked to be transferred to the Title 1 program, and I was assigned to teach at Warstler Elementary School. The principal and staff were great there.

I once again found I could use my creative energy. In the spring of each year, the school has a right-to-read program. One year I was asked to head that program. I thought of a way to combine reading with dance. It was a one-week program with an assembly on Friday afternoon. Each grade level was to read a book from a different country around the world. I decided to incorporate the setting of the book with a dance that was part of that country's culture. I invited students from each grade to volunteer to learn and perform that dance. So, if first graders read a book about Mexico, after a summary of the book was given at the assembly, students would perform the Mexican hat dance. Kindergarten did a simple African stick dance, while the older grade performed the Italian Tarantella, and another grade did the Greek Sirtaki dance. There were dances from England, Israel, Ireland, and the Cajun French culture performed. The students watching were so excited to see their classmates out there dancing. I received a lot of positive feedback.

In 2000, we moved up to Akron, and I started working at Woodridge Intermediate School. It was an interesting mix of students. The school was located in a rural town called Peninsula, but the students came from government housing in both Akron and Cuyahoga Falls, along with students who lived in and around the school, which was located on the edge of Cuyahoga National Park. One year, I decided to write a grant to bring the arts to the school. I felt most of the students attending our school had limited exposure to the arts. The grant was called the GAR Grant. After writing it, I was awarded funds to bring in an array of different performers and performances. I had the Akron Orchestra send a group to play; the University of Akron Quartet came as well as the Shakespearean Troupe from Columbus and a dance company from Cleveland. It's one thing to see these types of acts on television, but I felt that seeing them live was important for our students to witness and experience. While I was at Woodridge, the gifted teacher wanted to put on the play "A Midsummer Night's Dream" for the school. She asked if I would work with some students on dances to be performed between the acts. Since both my children were now older and on their own, I was able to stay after school and teach students who had signed up to learn the dances I choreographed. Once again, it gave me great satisfaction to be able to do this. Even in the classes, I found opportunities to broaden how students learn. After reading *The Enormous Egg* by Oliver Butterworth, I taught the fourth grade how to debate. The question the book posed was whether to keep a triceratops alive since it was beginning to cost taxpayers a lot of money. Both sides had to come up with arguments to defend their opinion. Watching this unfold is what gives a teacher fuel.

Although I did officially retire in February 2015, I found I wanted to teach at some level, so I decided to become a substitute. I enjoyed the opportunity to see what other educators were doing, and I ended up learning many new things. I had never taken a business class, and when I substituted at Parma High School, I was in a business law class, and I have to say it was very enlightening. At Aurora High School, I subbed for an English teacher who was teaching about the three different levels of friendship that were Aristotle's theory, utility, pleasure, and virtue. The class was reading *Of Mice and Men*, which was an example of utility. I later used this lesson when I got to teach full-time again. But the best opportunity I had while subbing was filling in for an art teacher at Crestwood High School in Mantua, Ohio, while she was preparing for her upcoming wedding. She had written a grant that was approved, allowing her to take some of her juniors and seniors to Scotland and Ireland over spring break to draw castles and cathedrals. Her goal in writing the grant was to give these students a way to create art portfolios that would give them a better chance to get into more prestigious art schools across the country. This is a small farming community in northeast Ohio, so this experience was going to be eye-opening for these students. She asked me to escort her and these students. I was more than happy to go. We did have a few parents who also came, but she, the other art teacher, and I were the only educators. The trip was great, and the students were wonderful. I love Edinburgh, Scotland, with its old castles and fairytale-like streets. While in Northern Ireland, we stayed in Belfast, which was also amazing. I loved the Titanic Museum. Dublin was a busy commercial city, but it had a youthful and joyful vibe. I was truly glad I got to see this part of the UK.

It's funny how life takes its twists and turns. You never know where you might end up. Never in my wildest dreams did I think I would end up living in California. I really thought I would spend the rest of my life living in Ohio and probably wintering in Florida. But in 2016, Perry made up his mind to take a position with a UCLA outpatient clinic up in Santa Clarita. He left in November of that year and got our apartment set up, and I joined him in mid-December. I had mixed feelings about the move. I hated leaving my daughter, and although my son was in New York, California seemed very far away from them. But on the other hand, I was excited for a new adventure.

Santa Clarita seemed like a nice place. It wasn't like being in the heart of Los Angeles. It was quite further northeast into the mountains. A much quieter place to live. What I enjoyed most about Santa Clarita were all the bike trails. However, I found it boring and needed to do something with my time. Once again, I decided I'd substitute. I looked online as to how to go about doing that and learned you needed to pass the CBEST. So, I got all my credentials together, and by February, I was subbing almost every day. I came back to Ohio for a few weeks in June and July. When I got back to Santa Clarita, I felt I needed to do more than substitute. I applied and got my California teaching credential in August. The following week I was offered a full-time teaching position to teach English and health at the L.A. County jail in Castaic. The program was called Five Keys. It was started in San Francisco and followed the SFSD's curriculum. The program was established as a way to cut the recidivism rate in California jails by offering inmates a way to earn their high school diplomas. The idea was that this would be a pathway for them to get better-paying jobs with a high school degree. The jail also offered college courses, and an instructor from the two-year College of the Canyons came in on Wednesday afternoons and taught two subjects. So, some of those inmates who did graduate with their high school diploma could also begin working toward a college degree.

The health classes I taught were a requirement for graduation. I had a lot more flexibility with the English classes. Each class ran for nine weeks. One time I taught a writing class. Sometimes I would be asked to teach a reading improvement course, and then there were times I'd teach an actual English lit course. Those were my favorites. I got to choose the theme and find books to go along with the theme. For example, during one of the nine weeks, we covered survival. We read and discussed the following books: *Night* by Eli Wiesel, *Into the Wild* by Jon Krakauer, *Surviving Hell, A POW's Journey* by Leo Thorsness, and *Lord of the Rings* by William Golding. In another English Lit class, I did the lesson I learned while subbing on friendship and looking at Aristotle's three types of friendships using books like *Of Mice and Men*, *The Kite Runner*, and *The Outsiders*.

Finally, I taught a unit on teaching history through song lyrics. Each student was assigned a particular song that related to something happening in American history. The students came up and spoke about their song and how it impacted our history, and then I played that song for everyone to hear. I tried to keep these songs in chronological order. We covered songs such as "The Night They Drove Old Dixie Down," "Sailing to Philadelphia" (which is about drawing the Mason Dixon line), "Fortunate Son" (about the Vietnam War), and "Hurricane Carter" (dealing with the racial tensions of the '60s). I had about twenty songs, and the students had to present a short explanation of why the song was written and its message. I think the students enjoyed doing something different, not realizing that they were writing, speaking, and analyzing.

One of the nicest things about this program is that Five Keys holds a graduation ceremony twice a year. The students get to invite one person from outside the jail to come and watch them march down in cap and gown to receive their diplomas. It's followed by a cake reception. These inmates who were permitted to partake in my classes were, for the most part, motivated to turn their lives around. Many were previously in gangs and had several tattoos. Some elected to go through with having their tattoos removed. It was also nice to see clergy coming in to give these men spiritual help.

Then one day a postcard came in our mail for Perry. It was announcing positions for internal medicine physicians for their 365 program at the Eisenhower Medical Center, which is located in Rancho Mirage, California. This is right next to Palm Desert, where Perry was originally hoping to find a job.

Perry had been thinking about leaving the UCLA medical system solely on the point that they did not give the physicians enough time to spend with their patients. I guess they were given only fifteen minutes for established patients and a half hour for new patients. Perry felt this was not sufficient to meet his patients' needs and, in some respects, was short-changing them. He was given a two-year contract, and he decided not to renew it.

So, when this notice came from Eisenhower Medical Center, he became very interested. He was now really into golf, and the Palm Desert area is a prime location for golf enthusiasts. It didn't take long after he applied to be offered a position.

We moved to Palm Desert in December 2018. During my first six months, I signed up for college courses at the California State University San Bernadino Palm Desert campus. The courses cost only eleven dollars for seniors. I also learned to play pickleball. Then, in the fall of 2019, I had the itch to teach again. So, I became a substitute for the Desert Sands Unified School District. Some days are more interesting than others. At this point, I'm not sure I can walk away from teaching. It's something I have been passionate about. It has given me a sense of fulfillment.

I feel teaching is an art because it requires skill, time, and patience. The artistry is in the way a teacher connects with the students and fosters their understanding. Starting the year is like a blank canvas. As the year progresses, color is brought onto the canvas, lighting up the scene. By the end of the term, the picture is complete. A beautiful masterpiece has been created. That is how I approach my profession. I am always excited about getting started and having a new group of learners to work with. Although I am given a curriculum, I craftily design how it will be taught and try to make the learning experience enjoyable while at the same time ensuring it will have a major impact.

FAMILY

The most important thing in my life is my family. Having a husband for a best friend makes me realize how lucky I am. He is always there to support and honor me.

I met Perry back in the summer of 1976. We were introduced to each other at a coffee house in Toledo, Ohio, by common acquaintances. Perry was on summer break after finishing his first year of medical school. I was living and teaching in Toledo. Although we did not date that summer, my girlfriends and I ran into him at the coffee house. At the end of that summer, before he went back to Guadalajara, Perry had a big house party. Many of his Ohio State University and Miami University friends attended. His mother and grandmother made a beautiful spread. It wasn't until the following year that things changed.

It was Memorial Day weekend, and my mother had come in to visit me. I took her to the pool at the Toledo JCC. While we were there, Perry and his friend Nick were just coming off the basketball courts and dribbling by us. I saw him and said hello. He stopped and began talking to me. Then he asked me for my phone number and address.

During that week, he actually stopped by my apartment. I was surprised to see him. He asked me out for the following weekend. Our first date was to a concert in the Detroit area. The band we went to see was The Marshall Tucker Band. I remember it being an outdoor venue. He picked me up in his father's big green Imperial. After the concert, he took me to a Greek restaurant in downtown Detroit. We dated that whole summer, and then he decided to take the fall semester off from medical school. While he was home, he worked in his father's furniture store, helping with the deliveries. Sometime in October, he took me to pick out an engagement ring at his parent's friend's jewelry store, Dolgin Jewelers. After a Halloween party we attended, he took me home and proposed. We got married the following July in New York.

My mother was adamant about having the reception at the Tavern on the Green in Central Park. Lucky for her, a couple, who were intending to marry there in July happened to cancel their reservation. My mother was able to book the wedding for July 9th, 1978. She also arranged to hold the ceremony at the Sutton Place Synagogue on 51st Street between 3rd Avenue and Lexington. The rabbi who married us was the brother of the infamous Meir Kahane, a member of the Israeli Knesset and a convicted terrorist. After the wedding, we decided to honeymoon in Toronto. On the way up to Canada, we stopped at Hammondsport, New York. It's on Keuka Lake, one of the finger lakes, and is known for its wine. Needless to say, after spending the day wine tasting, we were exhausted and ended up spending the night in a shabby motel in Buffalo. The next day we got to Toronto and had a wonderful time exploring the city. When we got back to the States, it was time to pack up and drive down to Guadalajara, Mexico. We spent one year there, one year on Staten Island, and then finally we moved back to Ohio in 1980.

I am grateful to have given birth to two healthy babies. Both of our children were born at Aultman Hospital in Canton, Ohio. I loved watching my daughter and son grow up to become the fantastic adults they are. It was exciting seeing my daughter, Leslie, perform on stage during dance recitals, in plays, and during the school Christmas pageant, playing her flute with the orchestra.

My son, Elliot, kept me busy with all the activities he participated in. There was never a dull moment. He played baseball, indoor and outdoor soccer, basketball, tennis, and even ice hockey. There was a time in middle school when he tried wrestling. Then, in high school, because we lived in the city of Akron, he and his best friend Sean were able to partake in free golf lessons at the First Tee program, located at the Mud Run Golf Course. It was from that experience that he became the great golfer he is today.

Education was always important to me. I went to every open house and parent-teacher conference that was held for my children. I also wanted my children to have a strong appreciation for Judaism. When we lived in Canton, there were very few Jews. There was a JCC, in which I had both children involved. The JCC offered swimming lessons, a summer camp, and tee ball. We did belong to a conservative synagogue, and my daughter had attended Sunday school and the community Hebrew school. I still felt it was inadequate. At about this time, Perry's father passed away in February of 1998. Perry was very close to his father, and his father's passing was hard on him. We had begun to attend an orthodox synagogue, and the rabbi there helped Perry through his grief. As a result, we started to become more observant. I even made my kitchen a kosher kitchen. Although we had to drive to the synagogue on Saturday, we spent the day there, learning with the rabbi. The children seemed to find friends there to play with, so it was really a nice way to spend the whole Saturday. After sundown, we'd go home and get ready to go out as a family for dinner.

The following fall, I enrolled my children in a Jewish day school up in Cleveland. It worked out well because they offered me a sixth-grade secular teaching position. This way I could drive my children, along with a few others, from Canton up to the school, which was an hour away. After one year, my daughter decided she didn't like going there because it was hard for her to maintain friendships while living so far away. We enrolled her in another Jewish day school when we moved to Akron, which she was much happier at. My son continued going with me up to Cleveland for one more year. The commute was really taking a toll on me. So, after two years, it was decided that my son, Elliot, would also go to the day school in Akron. I secured a teaching position closer to home, and everyone was happy.

We continued to be orthodox when we moved up to Akron in 1999. We joined an orthodox synagogue there and found a home located close enough so we could walk to services on Saturday morning. I stopped doing any housework on Saturday, and luckily, my son had many friends in the neighborhood that kept him busy. Leslie was on board for one year. She even had a beautiful Bas Mitzvah while she was in seventh grade. Once she started high school, it became clear that things would have to change. She joined the cross-country team, and the meets were on Saturday. Perry and I made the decision to go watch her. I also realized how difficult it was for me to try and do all the laundry and shopping on Sunday. Being a full-time teacher and maintaining a home with two children were wearing me down. Being orthodox was a commitment that we just could not logically abide by. Neither Perry nor I were raised in an orthodox home. We needed to find a comfortable compromise in dealing with our faith. We became traditionalists. We continued to attend the Orthodox synagogue, but we allowed the children to participate in any activities they wished to on Saturday, which included Elliot playing baseball and Leslie going shopping with her friends. As traditionalists, we celebrate all the

Jewish holidays, and I keep my kitchen kosher with separate dishes and flatware for meat and dairy.

The arts were also important to me. I wanted my children exposed to different forms of art. I looked for opportunities in the community that offered enrichment programs. When Elliot was about five, he took art lessons at the Massillon Art Museum. Leslie not only took dance lessons but also participated in theater productions at the Canton Public Library. Both children were in plays while they attended Lippman Day School, which I loved going to see.

While we lived in Canton, I learned that the McKinley Museum offered many exciting activities for children during the summer. Leslie got involved in some interesting science programs, which she seemed to enjoy.

When Elliot completed his junior year in high school, that summer he spent a few weeks at Hiram College studying drama. At the end of the program, the whole class performed a Shakespearean drama for the parents. Later that summer, he also went to Ithaca College in New York with his good friend Eli to work on sports writing.

Our family took many trips together. We'd go up to Toronto to see shows. One year we took our babysitter, Shirley, and she and Leslie went to see Phantom of the Opera. Our children also got to see the Lion King there. Another time we went to Montreal and Quebec City.

Whenever Perry had a medical conference, we made it a family vacation. We got to go to San Diego and stayed at the Coronado Hotel on Coronado Island. Before leaving San Diego, we took the children to the world-renowned San Diego Zoo and Sea World. Another time Perry had a conference in Santa Fe, New Mexico. We even brought my mother along. She had never been there and really wanted to go with us. I'm not sure how my children felt about this trip. But I, for one, loved it. I was so impressed with all the art that was displayed throughout the city. In the center of the city, there was a square where beautiful turquoise jewelry was being sold. There was also the Indian Museum, which chronicled the history of Native Americans throughout the country. It was an eye-opening experience for me. Finally, Perry and I got to go mountain biking for the very first time.

When the children got older, we traveled to Arizona two times. The first time was when Perry had a medical conference in Scottsdale, and the second time was for Elliot to check out Arizona State University (ASU) and the University of Arizona. He was interested in studying journalism, and ASU had the Walter Cronkite School of Journalism. The problem was that the school of journalism was in downtown Phoenix, and the main campus was in Tempe. We drove down to Tucson to visit the University of Arizona. I thought that the campus was beautiful. Elliot, after thinking about it, decided he wanted to go to The Ohio State University. His best friend was going there, and it was a lot closer to home. When Leslie was attending OSU between 2004 and 2008, Elliot would often go down to Columbus to attend football games with us. He also wanted to follow in his father's footsteps and join the Sigma Alpha Mu fraternity. In 2010, Elliot became a Buckeye.

Florida was our regular trip during winter and spring break. We'd go down and stay with my mother in Boca Raton. Sometimes we'd take an excursion to Orlando, and the children would go to Disney World, Magic Kingdom, Universal Studios, and Epcot.

These were fond memories. Now, as adults, both Leslie and Elliot seem to be well-rounded individuals with a strong appreciation of the world around them. They are both married now and have families of their own. I know they will continue to instill in their own children the important values they were brought up with.

My father Murray in his early twenties

My father with his parents,
Sam and Nora.

Mom and Dad on their
wedding day 6/23/1951

My mother as a teenager with her brother
Charlie, and parents, Julius and Anna

My mother holding me when I was an infant in 1953.

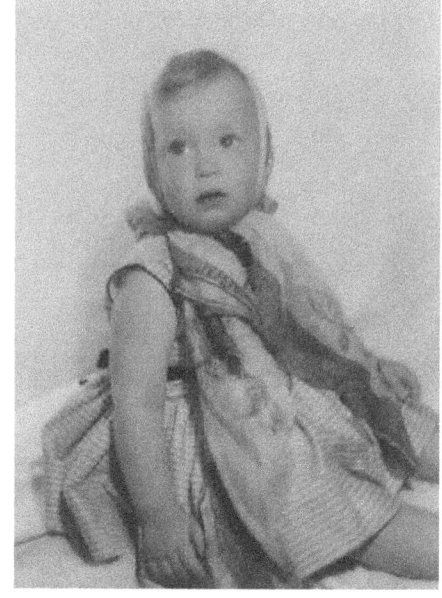

My baby picture at 10 months old.

Steven's Bar Mitzvah Day with Rick and our dog, Curly, the Airedale.

Rick's Bar Mitzvah Day 1969

Mom comes to Toledo to meet the Schall family, spring 1978.

A few days before my wedding in Glen Cove with my dad.

Richard and Mom right before our wedding ceremony, July 9, 1978.

Our wedding picture
July 9, 1978

The wedding party in front of Tavern on the Green. Rick, Mom, Linda Berg, and Rick Markoff.

Stopping at the wineries in Hammondsport, New York on our way to Toronto for our honeymoon.

Visiting the pyramids of the Sun and Moon near Mexico City., May 1979

FAMILY 87

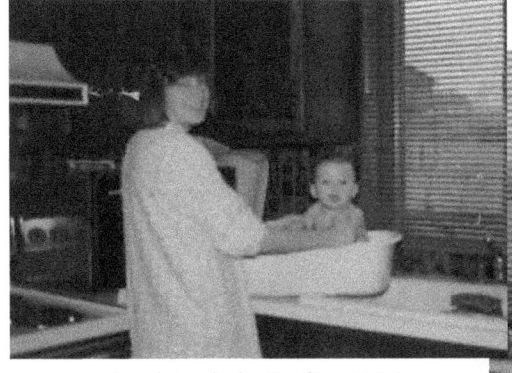

Bathing baby Leslie, 1986

Elliot at 10 months old, May 1993.

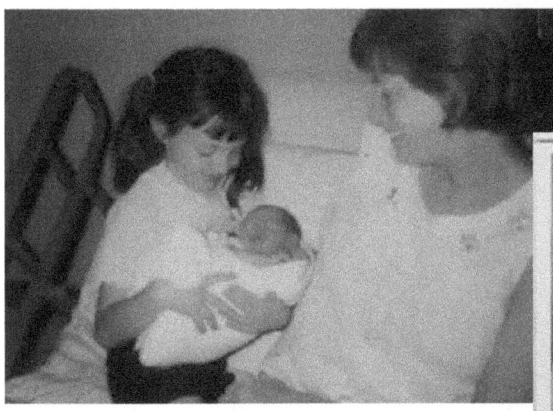

Elliot was born on July 6, 1992.

Family picture, Oct. 1994

Leslie's Bas Mitzvah, Feb. 1999

Elliot playing little league baseball in Akron.

Leslie playing softball on the Jackson Rec team, 1994.

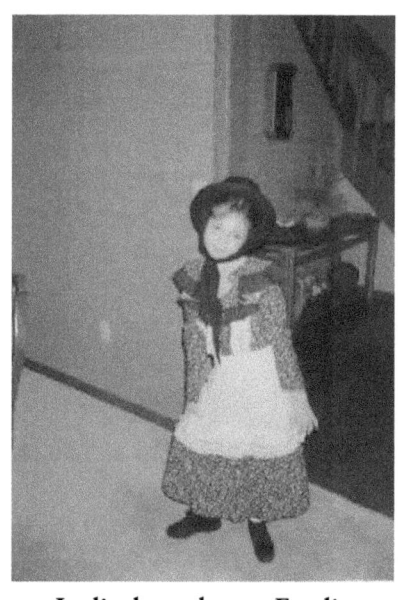

Leslie dressed up as Emelia Bedelia in 2nd grade.

Trip to Niagara Falls, 8/2000

Visiting Disney World, 12/1995

Family trip to Toronto. Dinner at
Gretsky's restaurant, May 1995

Leslie getting ready for her
flute recital, spring 1998.

Hanging out at Grandma Elaine's
pool in Boca Raton, Fla. 12/94

Miami Zoo Trip, 12/96

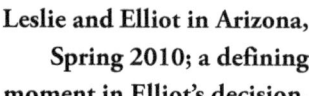

Perry and Me mountain biking in Sant Fe, 7/25/1995

Leslie and Elliot in Arizona, Spring 2010; a defining moment in Elliot's decision.

Grand Canyon, 3/28/2007

My mother getting ready for our trip to Ohio, 2011.

Murray and Ruth in North Miami in Jan. 1998.

Bella, my mother's loving dog.

Rosh Hashanah dinner at the Schall's Sept. 1983

Ben Schall at his 80th Birthday party, Dec. 1997.

FAMILY 93

Perry with his sisters Beverly and Andrea, and his mother Shirley Schall, Mother's Day 2007.

Me with my brothers, Steven and Rick

My brother Rick and sister-in-law Tracy.

Our family gathering in Woodstock, New York, July 2023.

Ella, Michael, Phoebe, and Leslie Kertesz.

Elliot, Jessie, and Jonah Schall.

Milton Keynes UK
Ingram Content Group UK Ltd.
UKHW021932130824
446844UK00012B/848